THE IRISH AT HOME

JANE McDONNELL & SARAH McDONNELL

Foreword by POLLY DEVLIN

GLOSS PUBLICATIONS

CONTENTS

FOREWORD

By POLLY DEVLIN

I grew up in Northern Ireland where the decorating ethic was kitchens is buff and landings is brown and where beauty in the house was regarded as an occasion of sin and decoration was as often as not a flickering light in front of an image of the exposed Sacred Heart. Perhaps as a consequence of this I have contrived to live in houses which I think are beautiful and which are crammed with things I love, havens where, surrounded by wonderful things imbued with the aura of previous times, I feel I could fulfill my life.

The Irish houses illustrated in these pages show something more than houses as a stage for self-fulfillment though that is there too. Edith Wharton wrote about how the creativity involved with her houses and gardens was essential to her, an act of self-definition, how she created in order to find her voice and, looking at these pages, one hears Irish voices coming through loud and clear. With one exception, all these houses are the creations of individuals done in their own time as expressions of their art in living, and that chimes with something I have always believed in particular about the Irish, that in making a beautiful house full of lovely things we are trying to compose and construct the semblance of our own lost disallowed Irish heritage, the aggregations that undisturbed or unvexed families in other countries with happier histories have passed down through generations. There is one such inherited house here in Clandeboye; the rest are unique individual creations filled with their owner's vision in a new Irish vernacular. It would be wonderful if they became Clandeboyes in their agelessness but the sad thing is that a beautiful interior is so ephemeral, so easily lost. Even in families who have lived in houses for generations the decoration of one generation, however inspired, is changed by the next. The great master of delightful, transient installation in the natural world is the bower bird which constructs elaborate and enticing bowers adorned with pebbles, feathers, shells, bits of glass "not as nests but as places of resort" and valuable territory. In the inspiring photographs here by the observant and unobtrusive Luke White these installations are preserved for posterity.

I once read two dry, little, unemphatic yet heart-breaking sentences in a history of Irish furniture by the great Claudia Kinmonth. There were descriptions of carvings on coffers or elm chests, representative of the kind of chest furniture found in Irish castles and lower houses until the Georgian period, but there were no examples of vernacular storage furniture. The sentence read, "The ownership of such articles or indeed the need for them, was confined to the landed classes. The destitution of the peasantry rendered storage boxes superfluous." In other words the Irish had nothing to store. Looking at these pages one can see how far we have travelled – these houses are stores of treasure, the results of avid and spectacular collecting, as well as architectural flights of fancy and ingenuity.

I hold that making your own environment beautiful is as valid a work of art as any piece of writing or painting; the handiwork, taste, inspiration and labour that go into the conception of a beautiful house or a pretty room are a major achievement, as one can see on every page here.

These pages cover such a range – the Irish abroad, delightful family homes, Dublin houses, restored country houses, houses treated with novel ideas. Each has its own spirit but one of the most delightful things to find in an interior is wit and David Collins' house sparkles with chic and wit as does Anne Madden's, the placing of whose remarkable contents are underwritten by her sharp artist's eye; the amazing sense of space in a small artisan's cottage with its Shaker-like bedrooms and pretty courtyard is impressive, as is the bravura of the colour and form of the contents of the Johnson house. All the houses and interiors here are sets which express drama, individuality and confidence and are the result of intellectual and aesthetic powers turned on building a setting and placing possessions in idiosyncratic and sweet decorum.

INTRODUCTION

In this book, we see inside 35 homes, some modest, some grand, a few significant landmarks, others off the beaten track, all lived in by Irish people. Some were badly in need of restoration when they were taken on by their owners, others were totally transformed from ugly ducklings into swans, others were conceived from scratch on the drawing board. Understandably reticent about revealing their own private spaces, the owners of these lovely properties often let us in, first to look, then to photograph, in order to help someone involved in the creation of their home, be they an architect, an interior designer, an artist or craftsperson, knowing that the exposure would be invaluable to them. We are grateful for that generosity: the range of interiors is impressive, given that as a people, in the past, we were not characterised by our love for interior decoration nor our ability to acquire valuable art and antiques. Although the last decade may be one some care to forget in terms of property, these houses demonstrate a lack of ostentation, a concern for appropriateness and an eye for the elegant, the eclectic, the interesting and the stylish. It is clear that an Irish home remains a place where the emphasis is on living well with family and entertaining friends and is not limited to the shade of wallpaper or provenance of a piece of furniture. There are handsome period houses in notable terraces, exquisite country houses, both old and new, and interesting and individual approaches to apartment living and urban design: a true reflection of how, as a nation, we like to live.

1

LIVING IN
AN IRISH CITY

If the cultural importance of Irish cities were to be measured by the calibre of inhabitants who contribute to the cities' social, cultural and economic development, then Dublin is rich indeed. Its diversity of building stock – Georgian streets and squares, Victorian retail buildings, artisan dwellings and contemporary apartments – has drawn many artists, designers, writers and poets and their homes, in turn, reflect their creative leanings with rooms filled with paintings, books, objects and furniture of interest. The typical city home is cosy, the eclectic interiors compensating perhaps for a reduced amount of terrace or garden space. There is always a table for family and friends to gather round and the fireplace is still the focal point. Daily life in an Irish city is relaxed – even in the cosmopolitan capital, everyone lives like a local.

ARTISTS IN RESIDENCE

HOW IRISH ART'S FIRST COUPLE MADE A HOME WITH THEIR WORK

Anne Madden and the late Louis le Brocquy, two of Ireland's most important artists, lived full time in Dublin from 2000, when they returned from a long exile in the south of France. They bought their first house in Dublin in 1978, and used it as a pied-à-terre but, when the adjacent house came on the market in the early 1990s, they made an offer and with the help of architect friend John Meagher, knocked the houses together and redesigned the interior. "Here we were in dirty old Dublin in a one-storey house, instead of a much bigger villa in sunny France, and yet it has the same feel," Madden says. The house is light and decorated with their own art, sculptures, and tapestries, and those of their friends too. Anne Madden describes her interiors style as putting the emphasis on "placing and spacing – like putting a big painting on a small wall". The furniture in the house looks well thought out, juxtaposing old and new, but Madden says, it's "a hotchpotch of Chilean, colonial French, Georgian and Edwardian, some pieces heirlooms, others acquired over the years." She adds, "It's a fluke that all the pieces work so well together, although it's very important to know what should go where." The main living area is a combination of modern – an original Mies van der Rohe Barcelona coffee table and two cantilevered leather chairs – and antiques, including a Victorian sofa reupholstered in white leather, draped with a black and white Chilean poncho, a George Hepplewhite antique desk and a simple rattan sofa. Barry Flanagan and Anthony Caro's sculptures sit on a George II sideboard, and an elegant side table, "La Table aux chats", by Diego Giacometti was a gift from the artist. Madden continues to paint at a studio near her house, but on summer days has lunch in the garden, which is small but planted with flowers and shrubs. Overlooking the garden is a conservatory filled with books and magazines – the perfect place for tea.

Previous page: On the wall opposite the front door, is one of Madden's paintings "Immolation" – from her Odyssey & Icarus series (1990-2000) – the colours she has used on this huge painting are powerful and mesmerising, a vivid gold sun image against an ultramarine background. The painting is perfectly hung above an elegant 1950s Knoll bench. *Above:* Anne Madden at home, in front of her work "Aurora Borealis 2", 2006. *Opposite:* The gilt mirror in the drawing room came from an antiques shop in Dublin. The tapestry is from Louis le Brocquy's Táin collection (1969-1999), ink drawings illustrating Thomas Kinsella's celebrated translation of the Irish epic.

Above and right: The Victorian sofa is upholstered in white leather. The Barcelona coffee table is by Mies van der Rohe. The desk is by George Hepplewhite. *Opposite:* The dining table and chairs are by Eero Saarinen and the mirror was bought in the 1950s at a French flea market.

Above: The antique desk is by George Hepplewhite. *Right:* The tapestry over the bed is "The Cherub" by Louis le Brocquy, 1952. Anne Madden designed the rugs as well as all the furniture in the bedroom. The sculptures in front of the bed are by Anne Madden, made by a process known as *cire perdue*.

CHARACTER STUDY

A DUBLIN HOUSE IS A BEAUTIFUL MIX OF ART, ANTIQUES AND MODERN DESIGN OBJECTS

Peter and Natasha Johnson's house in the heart of Dublin's south city, built in 1838, is arranged over two levels, and approached by a flight of granite steps to the first floor. When the Johnsons bought it in 1994, they set about getting the terrace listed. The couple completely rebuilt the front garden using Wicklow granite slabs, adding curved railings, raised beds and five exotic-looking "Moroccan pineapple" trees and a bronze sculpture by Tim Morris, Natasha's brother. The stylish exterior hints at something interesting within – and the interior does not disappoint. For Natasha, the last 20 years in the house, raising three children and seeing them move on to pastures new, have been very happy. "I just cannot believe our good fortune in having such an absolutely gorgeous house. Each time I open the front door, I get this incredible feeling of joy." Not surprisingly for a house owned by two artistic people – Peter is an interior designer and furniture collector and Natasha, a daughter of painter Camille Souter – the space reveals unexpected design touches and interesting pieces of furniture and objects acquired over 35 years. The upper floor comprises the more formal living room, principally used in winter, which can be entered by the original front door, a study and a large master suite. The living room opens via glass doors to the bright and airy study which overlooks the garden at the back. Both rooms have elegant fireplaces and are crammed with books and wonderful, mostly Irish, paintings and sculptures. Priority was given to the design of the master suite, which extends from the front to the back of the house. It is a spacious and very light arrangement: the bedroom is open to an elegant bathroom – there are no doors – and a four-poster bed by Duff Tisdall from the early 1990s is the focal point. Downstairs, a large kitchen and dining space leads into a home office and a cosy sitting room. French-style navy steel windows run the length of the kitchen-dining area and open to a wide pretty garden with a terrace.

Above: Peter Johnson at home. *Opposite*: Books, rugs and paintings in the study make for a warm and inviting interior. The chair and table in blonde wood and leather are by Bruno Mathsson. A number of Irish artists, including Patrick Scott, are represented in this room. The fireplace, original to the house, was once in the bedroom but was moved to the study and given a Regency inset.

Above: The door with fanlight leading from the living room once illuminated the otherwise dark hallway but is now incorporated into the living room. *Right:* The papier maché table was bought at the auction of the late Sybil Connolly's collection; the "Poet" sofa is by Finn Juhl; the chest is French reproduction. The standard lamp is chrome and leather and the table lamp, wood and bronze. Paintings include a collection by Irish painter Charles Brady, a nude by George Dawson and a Russian oil bought in London.

"The Bull" sculpture by Dick Joynt and paintings by Irish artists punctuate the drawing room space. The gilt ornamental mirror is Irish Regency and the ceramics by Irish artist John ffrench. The chair covered in navy and white fabric is Scandinavian. A French mirror hangs above an Irish table by David Deely. The sofa is by Peter Johnson Interiors.

Above: The main front door is rarely used, as family and visitors are drawn down the steps to the spacious entrance on the lower level with panelled door designed by Peter Johnson. Leading off the hall is lots of storage, a cloakroom and a guest bedroom. *Opposite*: In the open plan kitchen-dining area, the Danish dining table is surrounded by Danish dining chairs. The stone floor tiles are by Antica. The garden to the rear is wide and south-facing, with apple and cherry trees and two silver birches, a haven for bird life all year round. Amongst the flowers, there is a small kitchen garden. Note the Cumbrian canoe stored on the roof of the pretty garden shed.

Above: A mahogany bath surround and mirrors and "Psyche Au Bain" panoramic black and white wallpaper by Zuber in the bathroom add a fabulously luxurious touch. *Opposite*: The full-height headboard in an Italian chinoiserie fabric was made for the Duff Tisdall four-poster by Peter Johnson Interiors. The abstract painting is by Natasha Johnson's mother, Camille Souter. The chest of drawers on the right of the bed is Danish, made in the 1920s, and now reproduced by Peter Johnson Interiors. The blue wool carpet is by McMurray Carpets, Connemara.

A MEWS TO INSPIRE

AN ORIGINAL APPROACH TO A MEWS INTERIOR MARRIES OLD AND NEW

When antiques dealer Rosemarie McCaffrey departed Dublin for Santa Monica more than 20 years ago, she wanted to keep a Dublin base for herself and for her clients to stay in on trips to Ireland. She found a mews on a lane in Ballsbridge and engaged architect Ross Cahill O'Brien to create a space where she could entertain in some style and which would be a nice backdrop for her antiques. With all the period features of the original mews building obliterated, Cahill O'Brien made a decision to take most of it down and in the process uncovered – and was able to retain and restore – some of the original aspects and incorporate them into the new structure. A circular window and large arch, revealed as the bricks and mortar were dismantled, now lend elegance to the rear of the two-storey mews which faces south to a pretty courtyard into which a pond has been added. A rather surprising addition, this has had a dramatic effect both inside and out. Instead of looking over a small garden, visitors find themselves drawn to walk around it and when it rains, a spout fills the pond, an event in itself according to the owner. It creates very nice reflections on the walls of the interior, especially in the dining area. The open plan ground floor, with custom-made signature panelling by Ross Cahill O'Brien, has a double-height ceiling with a fine steel staircase, inspired by the old Victorian structures of the 19th-century, which leads to a mezzanine library off which are two bedrooms and a bathroom. The contemporary elements of this design are all characterised by their craftsmanship, equal to the impact made on the space by a beautiful collection of antiques.

Above: A small lobby opens to the open plan ground floor space where the workmanship of a contemporary Bulthaup kitchen looks cool amongst the period pieces. *Opposite:* The staircase, made as lightweight as possible to minimise its volume, has a short run of marble steps leading to bleached maple slats which are bolted together and a narrow metal handrail with thin steel wires. The Provençal buffet with stone top is late 19th-century with a painting of Montmartre above. The bergère chairs are Louis XVI with 19th-century needlepoint cushions.

Above: A pivoting doorway opens from the dining room to the small garden with pond. The pretty arch to the right was revealed during building work and incorporated into the new design. *Opposite:* The mezzanine is a light-filled gallery space, the shelves crammed with books. A lectern is built into the rail. The floor is slatted to allow light permeate downstairs.

Above: In the bathroom, an antique mahoghany cabinet is a table de chevet or night table. The contemporary Villeroy & Boch basin and chrome shower with panelling runs flush to the floor, keeping the look simple and streamlined. *Left:* The bedroom with Italian hand-carved bedhead upholstered in vintage fabric; the walnut chest is French 19th-century; the painted chest is Italian 19th-century. The high corner window provides great light without compromising privacy.

STARTING OVER

A REMODELLED COTTAGE STAYS FAITHFUL TO ITS VICTORIAN HERITAGE

Faced with the task of gutting and rebuilding an existing period house, the temptation is often to start from scratch on the inside and go for something radically different, but when renovating this cottage on the banks of Dublin's Grand Canal, the owner's priority was to preserve the original Victorian character while putting his own stamp on it. When he acquired the house, which dates from 1867, it consisted of just two bedrooms and a living room – there was no bathroom. A design by David Averill of Sheehan & Barry architects solved the spatial challenges by cleverly adjusting the size of the bedrooms to create space for a generous bathroom, increasing the overall size of the dwelling to 67 square metres. The original living area became a monochrome kitchen, while what was once the yard was converted into a light-filled, high-ceilinged living room, leaving space for a small garden at the back. Fortunately, despite decades of wear and tear, the original floors and fireplaces survived, and some salvage work restored them to near mint condition. In the living room extension, the new floorboards were treated to match the originals, creating a sense of continuity between the old and new parts of the house. The structure complete, the owner set about furnishing it with a nod to the house's period heritage – traditional with a contemporary edge – and the resulting mix of modern and Victorian furniture is a testimony to his eclectic taste and expert eye. Decorating as he went along, he furnished the house almost from scratch, putting the pieces from his previous modern apartment into storage. In the kitchen, a Victorian dining table and reproduction chairs face an Eileen Gray side table; classic Irish pieces include a traditional hallstand, found in Enniscorthy, and the Victorian bed in the guest bedroom. The colours throughout are by Farrow & Ball, muted shades of grey, chalk and eau de nil that enhance the quietly cool mood and allow the house's – and owner's – character make the impression.

Above: The front garden of the Victorian terrace was designed by Landscape Restoration. *Opposite*: In the living room – a light-filled space extending into the original back garden – a large storage cupboard designed by the Victorian Salvage Company conceals the television and sound system. The floor here was treated to match the original elsewhere in the house.

Above: A quiet patio space at the back of the house is accessed via the guest bedroom through French doors; imaginative planting makes the most of the small area. *Opposite*: The black and white kitchen, with polished granite worktops, occupies the original living area. Vintage posters and an eclectic mix of furniture reflect the owner's taste – including an original Victorian dining table and an Eileen Gray chrome side table.

Left: The bathroom, with its freestanding roll-top bath, was created by the clever redistribution of space from the two bedrooms.

Above: A series of framed album covers runs along one wall.

Above: In the guest bedroom, a Victorian bed is in keeping with the period of the house. *Right:* The master bedroom, at the front of the house, features a salvaged fireplace and recessed shelving. Minimal artwork and a cool palette reinforce the restful mood.

PERFECTLY FORMED

THE DEMANDS OF A SMALL CITY COTTAGE ALLOWED ITS OWNER TO THINK BIG

When furniture designer Simon O'Driscoll came into possession of this charming artisan cottage near Dublin's Portobello, it was a modest single-storey dwelling in need of a complete overhaul and some fresh thinking. Luckily, O'Driscoll comes from a family of visionaries, and with the help of his architect brother Micheál, the original building was demolished and rebuilt, nearly doubling in size to 70 square metres. The six-month rebuild opened it up to create a light-filled modern living space, with the addition of a second floor. Clean and uncontrived, with an emphasis on beautiful materials, the new cottage was the perfect showcase for O'Driscoll's collection of contemporary furniture. This includes both classics – an Eames Aluminium Group Lounge chair in the main living area – and pieces he has designed with brother Tadgh, like the white oak DC dining chairs, originally created as part of a line of furniture for Dublin City University, and a walnut and coloured steel kitchen table. The uniformly off-white walls allowed O'Driscoll to introduce bold splashes of colour through pieces such as the red Studio sofa and orange Zoon chair and stool and carefully chosen art, like the original Calder poster in the kitchen. Unsurprisingly, the attention to detail is meticulous, be it the finish on a surface or the angle of a step, and the variety of timber used throughout – iroko, black walnut, ebony, bamboo, Douglas fir – reflects a purist's approach to materials. Further putting his mark on the interior, O'Driscoll designed and made the kitchen units himself – doors of dark wenge veneer under a Carrera marble countertop, with further marble tiling on the wall. When rebuilding, O'Driscoll's main concerns were light and space and to this end, the front window was enlarged to let in more daylight. In extending upwards, space was created for a new bedroom and a generous-sized gleaming bathroom – all mirrors and white mosaic tiling – while downstairs, a study at the back of the house occupies the space of the former bedroom. Here, the print by Irish artist John Graham came from the Green on Red gallery, owned by yet another O'Driscoll brother, Jerome. While small in size – though without a centimetre wasted – this beautifully put-together home reflects not just a designer's eye for detail and material, but also the breadth of Irish creative talent, in art, architecture and design.

Above: Simon O'Driscoll at home. To his left, Roy Lichtenstein prints. *Opposite:* The owner and his architect brother demolished and rebuilt the original cottage to create an open, airy living room and kitchen, and added an extra storey to house the bedroom and bathroom. Design classics sit alongside O'Driscoll's own pieces of furniture.

Above: In the study to the rear of the ground floor, an ebony veneer glass-topped desk and original Eames LCW lounge chair in plywood. *Opposite*: Off-white walls allow boldly coloured furniture and accessories to take centre stage; in the living room, the red Studio sofa, orange Zoon chair and stool and a yellow acrylic bowl, originally a one-off design commissioned for the National Concert Hall, are all by O'Driscoll Furniture.

Above: O'Driscoll's Armitage day bed with the figure of a woman stitched into the fabric occupies the space under the black walnut staircase by Ebony & Co. *Opposite*: Art plays a significant role throughout; the print over the fireplace is an original artist's proof, bought at a market in New York, while a print by Irish artist John Graham hangs to the right.

2
NOVEL APPROACHES

The transforming powers of the architect and interior designer were explored to the full in Ireland during the Celtic Tiger years when it seemed no site was too challenging, no space too awkward, no cost too high to be addressed. But it wasn't only the projects at which money was thrown that we now appreciate for their invention. Many of the most interesting spaces are examples of clever problem-solving, of ingenious rethinking of layout and of adventurous ideas about structure and materials, rather than of extensive budgets. The selection over the following pages is made by focusing on a common theme, that of the novel approach to issues that may be simply about form and function or how to deliver a design that can satisfy all the conditions of the planners yet provide the kind of living conditions required by the owner. And yet each unique home is a reflection of the owner's own openness to radical thinking, to rising to the challenge and taking the alternative route. Even those unaccustomed to embracing the new confessed delight in having the confidence to step outside their comfort zone.

DUBLIN UNDERGROUND

A PAIR OF UNIQUE HOUSES IS THE RESULT OF SIX YEARS
OF INGENUITY AND ARCHAEOLOGY

Now home to perhaps Dublin's most ingenious pair of houses, a parallelogram-shaped plot at John Dillon Street in the heart of the Liberties is part of the garden of the church of St Nicholas of Myra (aptly the patron saint of property owners as well as being Santa Claus). When the site came up for sale over a decade ago, architect Tom de Paor was approached to make a planning application on behalf of a consortium who wanted to sell it on with planning – he then decided, with Jay Bourke, to develop the plan himself resulting in the building of two unique houses – 0 and -1 John Dillon Street. The address says it all – the houses are secreted from the streetscape of one-storey cottages behind a stone wall punctured only by a subtle sliding cedar panel. As the plot was in the grounds of a listed cathedral, a lengthy excavation revealed 13 burial chambers and two unlined charnel pits and an archaeological dig uncovered artefacts and environmental material dating from the 13th century. With discoveries complete, two-storey shot-blasted concrete volumes were poured into the deep pit of a site, resulting in a pair of courtyard houses that are toplit – the living spaces are all about the sky. Street entry to the houses via the sliding cedar panel in a concrete niche in the stone wall is to a suspended half landing of No 0, sister house to No -1 next door. The eye is drawn in different directions: to bright living spaces on different levels, sliding glass panels revealing joinery made from recycled timber, to the communal roof terrace of blue marram grass designed and planted by Andrew Vickery, to expanses of marble – Carrera and Connemara – both inside and out, to the Harry Clarke stained glass window and the cupola of the church of St Nicholas of Myra. This excavated world is all connected: internal partitions are glazed and slide, all floors, beds and tables are hardwood decks. Tom de Paor has achieved a fine balance between concealment and revelation, entertainment and retreat, between the old and the new.

Previous page: The kitchen with recycled joinery. *Above*: The terrace, garden and top meadow courtyard with cast-iron steps over the skylight. *Opposite*: The table and sliding wall frame the garden. The turned plywood bowl is by Tony Cullen.

Above: The view to the Connemara marble-lined Jacuzzi which is open to the elements. *Opposite*: The terrace and living room bathed in light from the south. The chair and footstool are by Marcel Breuer.

Above: The master bedroom connects with the Jacuzzi and the second bedroom. *Opposite*: The burgundy recliner is by Jasper Morrison, the lamp by Achille Castiglioni.

Above: The tokonoma above the entrance is a place for favoured things, in this case some soldiers in cast plaster and plastic, a found conch and a Chinese doll. *Opposite*: Shuttering holes in the concrete allow for hanging pictures. The white ottoman is by Antonio Citterio and the red Tempo table is by Prospero Rasulo.

BRIGHT IDEA

INVENTIVE USE OF LIGHT AND SPACE GIVES A CITY HOME AN AIRY FEEL

When an apartment in a 19th-century carriage house in Dublin went on the market some years ago, the potential owners loved its prime position but not the characteristics of its 1980s-style conversion, so they commissioned architect-turned-design consultant, Clodagh Nolan, to transform it into the perfect town pied-à-terre. She restructured the space and devised a new layout encompassing two bedrooms and bathrooms, an open plan living space and study, and all within 89 square metres. Apart from lovely restored sash windows and the chimneypiece wall, which she retained, other 1980s additions were removed and freestanding and curved walls were added to separate living from sleeping areas. The entire space was remodelled to give a more modern feel: doors that were taller than the norm were used and cornices and skirtings removed so walls were flush with the pale oak floor. The apartment is entered via a small hallway at ground level where, at the foot of an angled stairs to the first floor, a practical utility space was fashioned. Upstairs, a study-cum-third bedroom is on the left beside a shower room and ahead, a curved wall leads to the right from where the entire apartment can be seen. The smaller of the two bedrooms is first, then the kitchen, occupying a central position and accessible from both sides of the space, making it a genuine hub. The neat design maximises height to create high-level storage and the absence of doors boxing it off means that although the kitchen is compact, it doesn't feel hemmed in, even when guests come to dinner. Next is the living area, a seemingly large and airy space, Nolan's aesthetic of combining light and volume making it appear twice its actual size. Greenery can be seen in every direction through the windows with their newly customised concertina shutters – the only window dressing. Still a focal point, the original chimneypiece wall now contains a smaller fireplace opening with a simple limestone surround. A wall of storage provides a home for books and the clients' collection of porcelain. The space achieves a simple harmony with a palette of sage green and celadon grey with touches of lilac and plum. The soft, restful scheme is given an edge by well-chosen materials in furniture and fittings – aluminium, glass mosaic, stainless steel, concrete, pale oak and ceramics – and the pieces of Irish art in every room.

Above: A feeling of openness in the relatively small space is evident in the living room, where a harmonious palette of cream and heather enhances the tranquil mood. *Opposite*: White painted walls and wooden floors are the starting point for the apartment's clean design, with a series of windows letting light pour in.

Above and opposite: A unified colour scheme gives a sense of coherence to the overall design. In the kitchen, the clever space solutions extend to ceiling-level cupboards for long-term storage, and recessed shelving to either side of the dining table and chairs.

Above: Glass mosaic tiles and a simple Linea Beta sink in the bathroom. *Opposite*: In the master bedroom, white walls and bedlinen create a restful mood. The customised concertina shutters are the only window dressing throughout the apartment.

NEW AND IMPROVED

A DYNAMIC DESIGN AND A SMART RETHINK GAVE THIS DUBLIN APARTMENT A NEW LEASE OF LIFE

Too often, when we think of modern interiors, the first thing to spring to mind is something minimalist, cool – cold, even – but when architect Damien Murtagh was approached to redesign a two-bedroom apartment in Ballsbridge, his vision was for a home that would be warm and congenial, yet utterly contemporary. He started by completely rearranging the layout, with the owner's blessing, in order to make the most of the relatively compact area (80 square metres) and incredible views – the apartment is on the building's sixth floor, overlooking the city as far as the Wicklow Mountains on one side, and the sea on the other. To this end, the existing entrance hall and second bedroom were done away with, freeing up space to create an open plan living/dining/kitchen area, with one bedroom and two bathrooms. This immediately gave an impression of extra space, letting light pour in and providing unbroken vistas through the glazed external wall, without the interference of partition walls. The real innovation, however, was Murtagh's design for a sleek, curved system of panels in the main living area, in elegant masur birch, which would fulfill a variety of functions. Built by Fitzgerald's of Kells, what appears at first to be a wood-panelled wall actually incorporates shelving, a sliding screen, a concealed bathroom door, a wardrobe and drinks cabinet, as well as housing more prosaic items like the hot water tank. It was a bold solution to the storage challenges presented by the loss of the second bedroom, but as well as serving practical functions, the panels' golden tones and decorative grain create interest and warmth, while cherrywood parquet flooring enhances the sense of luxurious comfort. Recessed spotlights and lengths of white, red and yellow tube lighting, cleverly concealed by curved ceiling panels, bathe the interior with a gentle, pinkish light. The walls throughout are white stucco, their matte finish a nice textural counterpoint to the sheen of the birch. For the bedroom, with its ensuite travertine marble bathroom, Murtagh designed wardrobes in frosted glass and maple, once again demonstrating his devotion to natural materials. This room is separated from the main area by a sliding screen, maintaining the sense of openess and fluidity while allowing for privacy when necessary. This is typical of the architect's sensitive, ingenious approach – one which has transformed this apartment from the inside out.

Above: The curved façade of the apartment block. *Opposite*: The brown leather armchair and sofa enhance the sense of warmth and comfort created by the cherrywood flooring and masur birch system of panels. A sliding screen separates the bedroom from the living room.

Above: Murtagh's devotion to natural materials is evident everywhere: the work surfaces of the kitchen by McNally Living are polished granite. *Opposite:* The elegant birch panel system fulfills a multitude of storage functions, while yellow and pink tube lighting, cleverly concealed in the ceiling, casts a warm glow.

Above: The floor-to-ceiling windows mean the space is bathed in light all day long. *Opposite*: In the bedroom, the wardrobes, also designed by Murtagh, are made from maple and frosted glass. The travertine wall and floor tiles in the bathroom are from Antica.

VIEW FROM THE TOP

A DOCKLANDS PENTHOUSE IS THE PICTURE OF URBAN COOL

When Jessica McCormack took on the job of designing the interiors for a Clarion Quay penthouse, she had a phenomenal blank canvas to work with. The split-level apartment, which occupies the entire seventh floor of one of the complex's three towers, has breathtaking views of the city's skyline, suffused with light throughout the day, and with a twinkling backdrop at night-time. Given the atmospheric charge this lends the space, McCormack's task was to create calm, neutral interiors with a contemporary edge that would balance the drama of the views – a tranquil eyrie from which to survey the city below. Given the apartment's airiness and unparalleled location, architects Urban Projects wisely left the layout relatively simple and uncluttered, heightening the sense of space – an entrance hall leads on to a double-height living area, which comprises a seating and dining area with glazed walls allowing stunning views to the east, west and south. McCormack, who was involved from early on in the project, designed the interior scheme with an awareness of the architectural elements rather than simply dressing the space. There is a fluidity to the layout of the main living area, which makes the most of the open space: the compact kitchen is separated from the dining area by a breakfast bar; at the other end is a study with a sliding door to close it off from the main area when required. The two bedrooms – a master suite, and a second smaller room – are also on this level, each with its own bathroom. Upstairs, a gallery looking onto the roof garden is a quiet, contemplative space, but the real star is the garden room, an indoor/outdoor space between the gallery and the garden. On one side, the glazed wall separates it from the main living area, while a glass door opens to the east-facing balcony. Echoing the floating feeling of the space itself is the Eero Aarnio bubble chair which McCormack had installed – the perfect place to curl up with a book and take in the ever-changing light of the city sky.

Above: The docks, quays, warehouses and slick contemporary towers of the Dublin docklands skyline. *Opposite*: The iroko-clad gallery and garden room, opening on to the roof terrace, glow in the evening light.

Above: A breakfast bar separates the dining area from the kitchen, with its maple units and granite worktops. *Opposite*: In the garden room, it's all about light: the Eero Aarnio bubble chair is suspended from the ceiling, its transparency allowing light in from all directions. Even with the huge doors open to allow in the hum of docklands traffic, special acoustics within the bubble swallow the sound.

Left: Upstairs, the gallery is a quiet space for hanging out; the windows and doors throughout are of untreated iroko. *Below left:* The apartment is entered via a private lift lobby. The bedrooms lead off the spacious entrance hall, which opens on to the main living and dining space. *Below right:* The open plan living and dining area is ideal for entertaining. *Opposite:* Most of the furniture in the living area was sourced at Minima, with a console and shelving unit creating a clever cocktail bar under the staircase. In the background, separated by a sliding door, is the study.

DESIGN FOR LIFE

CLEVER FURNISHING PROVIDED THE KEY TO PUTTING AN INDIVIDUAL
STAMP ON A TYPICAL TWO-BEDROOM DUBLIN APARTMENT

The appeal of modern apartment living is easy to understand – clean and convenient, a new build offers owners a completely fresh start with no need for months of costly renovation. The challenge often comes, however, when trying to create that sense of individuality and "character" we associate with period homes, and it's something Robert Trench has achieved brilliantly in his third-floor apartment in a modern building in Inchicore. Rather than letting the space dictate the style of décor, Trench took his lead from the furniture he had already accumulated over several years, some of it picked up on travels abroad – like the rug in the bedroom from Turkey – some sourced during his long career in design and interiors. The living room, to the right off the L-shaped entrance hall, benefits from the corner location, with an abundance of light pouring in on two sides. This gave Trench more freedom when choosing colours, allowing him to opt for shades of taupe that might have looked drab in a darker space; as it is, the colour of the walls changes subtly throughout the day according to the shifting light, with the oak floors lending an added warmth. One of the few pieces bought specifically for the apartment was the Greg sofa by Zanotta which, along with the Eileen Gray-designed rug, sets the contemporary tone. Another key element is the white Haller modular storage system by USM, which Trench already owned. Originally a single cabinet, additional units were added to create a long, low sideboard for books and framed photographs. The art, too, is an imaginative mix of photography, architectural prints and paintings – much of it by Irish artists, and some picked up at graduate shows. In the living room, the series of framed storyboards from the battle scene of *Braveheart* provide a clue to the owner's previous career in the film industry. Down the corridor are the two bedrooms, one of which has been converted into a dining room – Trench, a keen host, was adamant that there be space for small dinner parties with friends.

Above: Robert Trench. *Opposite*: The apartment is on the southwest corner of an apartment building, and the living room benefits from light throughout the day. The owner's background in design is evident through pieces like the Bertoia wire chairs and the rug, an Eileen Gray design.

Opposite: The Greg sofa by Zanotta in the living room was one of the few pieces bought specifically for the apartment. In front of it is a Ligne Roset coffee table. *Above*: In the dining room (originally a second bedroom), a smart Bulthaup table and Eiffel chairs by Charles and Ray Eames keep the space clean and uncluttered. The soldier figures were picked up at a NCAD graduate show.

Above: Although the apartment is predominantly contemporary in mood, more traditional pieces provide an interesting counterpoint, like the inlaid cabinet that Trench found in a bric-a-brac shop on Camden Street, the architectural prints, and a rug bought in Turkey. *Opposite*: Texture, from the perspex Ligne Roset bedside table to the inherited fur blanket, is key in the bedroom, with the artwork adding colour to a restrained palette.

DOWNSTAIRS, UPSTAIRS

THIS VICTORIAN TERRACED HOUSE IN NORTH DUBLIN
IS A SURPRISE ON MANY LEVELS

Built in 1879 and redesigned in the 1990s by architect Tom de Paor, this house became the architect's family home until the attraction of a bigger space and a leafier location beckoned. When he acquired it, the once corner shop had become a wholesale electrical shop which he then proceeded to domesticate, re-defining the spaces and reconfiguring the rooms to communicate with each other in more interesting, even novel, ways. There is little, other than some partially opaque glazing, on the outside to suggest the inventions within this two-storey over basement structure: the front door opens to a landing with a shallow stairs drawing the eye downstairs to a long dining and living space and kitchen, the stained mahogany joinery used on the stairs, floors, walls and windows making the tall house feel integrated, like a wooden cabinet occupying the old period brick shell. Although below ground, the dining space to the rear benefits from a retracting glass screen to the small walled garden, allowing in lots of light, whilst at the opposite end, the dark wood kitchen opens to a tiny courtyard in which a single tree can be seen through the tiny window. Upstairs, in the library, three steps lead to the stairwell and the bathroom, the sunken bath aligned with a floor-to-ceiling view of the pergola in the walled garden. The bathroom door closes to become the shower screen. Then, there is the unique take on the lavatory, a cabinet overlooking the bath below; then above and beyond, the bedrooms, with skirtings and architraves picked out in paint colours that complement the walls. In all, the architect has devised eight levels of accommodation from top to bottom, an unconventional response to inner city living.

Above: Tom de Paor in his former house. *Opposite*: The library/sitting room, formerly the shop, with aperture leading to the bathroom. The silkscreen is by Bridget Riley, gesso painting by Chung Eun Mo and moquette by Maud Cotter. The tweed and chrome chair is by Eero Saarinen, the coffee table by Charles and Ray Eames.

Left: In the bedroom, a 1960s pink leather armchair, a photograph on aluminium by Rut Blees Luxembourg, and Donegal tweed curtains. *Right*: The kitchen with sapele mahogany cupboards and stairs, stacking fibreglass chairs by Charles and Ray Eames, table by Alvar Aalto and, to the right, a photograph of Francis Bacon's kitchen by Perry Ogden. *Below*: The living area with sofa by W Landels and paper lamp by Isamu Noguchi. The floor is Carrera marble.

Above: In the bedroom, a Paul Seawright photograph on aluminium and a Gae Aulenti lamp on an inverted Corinthian timber column. The chrome mirror folding screen is 1920s American and the bedspread is by Foxford. *Opposite*: In the courtyard, a 1960s Danish easy chair, seastones, mirror and a Japanese maple.

3

IRISH FAMILY HOMES

The Irish family home has in recent years undergone a transformation from a purely functional place to live to a well-planned, light-filled space adapted to the needs of the family who resides there. In the houses in this chapter, restorations, new builds and, in one case, the two, neatly stitched together, family comes first, with informal spacious kitchens and living rooms at the heart of each home, where the whole clan can gather, and rooms dedicated to grown-ups, where peace reigns. All the homes reflect the families' personalities and in the case of the period homes, show a sensitivity to the original design and a sense of adventure when it comes to extending. One project began with a complete overhaul of wiring and plumbing in a derelict house – undaunted, the owners proceeded and have spent enjoyable years evolving the stage on which their busy lives unfold. As for decorating, the owners, some with experience of living in other countries, have confidently mixed the contemporary and the antique, grafting their own style onto homes which function brilliantly, and yet retain character and charm. Outdoor spaces and gardens are thoughtfully integrated, providing yet more functional – and attractive – space. Each home is a labour of love, and a unique place in which to play, live and relax.

THE WHITE HOUSE

A LIGHT AND FRESH INTERIOR MAKES A SUNNY FAMILY HOME

In 2003, Miriam Peters' rather dilatory house-hunting plans took on a whole new urgency when she and her husband Nigel Bray viewed a two-storey semi-detached Victorian house with coach house, built around 1862, close to their existing home. In spite of its rundown state and the fact that it had been chopped up into apartments in the 1940s, they fell in love with it immediately. It was an unusually decorative house, the predominant architectural style to the front is described as "Venetian Gothic", probably influenced by Ruskin, with its balcony on the piano nobile, and a decorated gothic arched entrance. Her plans to renovate started to take shape that same evening. Determined to have it, she engaged architect Paul Brazil to advise on the extent of work required and, still prepared to undertake the major renovation prescribed, made a successful bid at auction. For Peters, being in the business of restoring and renovating houses for clients both in Ireland and abroad (she is owner and founder of the Minnie Peters interiors business), it was a dream come true. She knew how she wanted the house to be and how to achieve it. With a new baby and another on the way, the couple wanted the house to be an informal family home, yet smart enough to be a showcase when clients needed to see her work in situ. As it was a protected structure, plans for the house would need to be made in agreement with the authorities, and sensitive to the fabric of the house. While the rooms were certainly spacious enough, especially the large hall and living room, the house was found wanting in certain critical areas. The first step was to extend at the back to create a kitchen-cum-family-dining area, and then to connect this with the drawing room to allow effective flow throughout the ground floor. Plans for a glazed passageway at the rear of the house were devised, allowing the kitchen-dining area to link with the drawing room: this has turned out to be one of the nicest aesthetic aspects of the house and a stunning addition to the view of the house from the garden. The build took two years, with Peters acting as project manager on the dust-laden construction site practically every day. The interior has a relaxed, unstuffy atmosphere with a mixture of old and new furniture, mirrors and objects.

Previous: The dining room with Moissonnier table. *Above*: Miriam Peters at home. *Opposite*: Throughout, the palette is gentle – white, dove grey and soft khaki. Painted furniture in tones of grey from steel to off-white is both elegant and practical. In the hall, a cabinet provides lots of storage.

Above: Black and white photographs (here, of Peters' daughter) are hung throughout. *Right*: The drawing room, with ornate cornicing and new double doors that open to a glazed link which leads to the kitchen. The large torchère floor lamp is French and the table lamp with zinc base is from Belgium. The bookcase was chosen specially for its height and drama. The overmantel mirror with its narrow frame was designed to fit.

Above: In the kitchen, steps lead to the glazed link. A caryatid is mounted on a reclaimed wooden plaque. *Left:* The Chalon kitchen with large maple-topped island. The linen curtains are faded khaki to blend with the colour of the French doors. One of Miriam Peters' many visits to antique fairs yielded the pair of French antique lights. *Opposite:* The dining room, linked to the drawing room by double doors, has a Moissonnier central pod dining table (which can extend to seat up to ten people) and Massant calico-covered dining chairs in an antiqued grey finish. The bookcase is fitted with library lights.

Above: In the master bedroom, cream silk curtains are hung at the floor-to-ceiling height windows. The bed and daybed are by Massant. *Opposite*: The bathroom-cum-dressing room with bleached herringbone oak parquet floor and antique teardrop chandelier.

AN OBJECTIVE VIEW

A SOPHISTICATED MIX OF EAST AND WEST MAKES AN INTERESTING HOME
FOR THE AMERICAN OWNERS OF THIS DUBLIN PERIOD HOUSE

When the owners of this south county Dublin Victorian terraced house took possession, they had to undertake a major purge of their extensive collections of Asian, European and American objects and art. Having lived in a larger space abroad for a number of years, they welcomed the opportunity to hone their collection of belongings so that only the finest pieces were kept. Almost a decade living in Ireland meant their interest in contemporary Irish art was piqued so that the interior that resulted is a delightful mix of east and west, old and new. Spared having to deal with the stress of renovating, thanks to the work completed by the previous owners, an upgrade of kitchen and bathrooms and a decision to decorate throughout in one go rather than piecemeal, meant that the approach to hanging their paintings and placing their objects was thoughtful, cohesive and considered. A neutral background was agreed, with Powdering Snow by Colortrend used in almost every room and the pitch pine floorboards throughout were exposed, varnished, then partially covered in carefully chosen rugs by Peter Linden and Louis de Poortere. The sitting room, with drapes in Colefax and Fowler's Montrose silk and chairs upholstered in Dae silk by Manuel Canovas, opens to the dining room with its American Century dining table and chairs and a display of carved Chinese panels on the walls. The lamps, in salvaged rosewood, were bought in Francis Street. Upstairs on the landing, an elephant chair from Thailand, upholstered in Ralph Lauren's Delamotte Stripe, makes the perfect daybed. The bedrooms are elegant: the master bedroom with its dark woods, bedlinen by Frette, reclining buddha and paintings by Michael Mulcahy and contemporary American artist, Greg Caliby opens to a pretty ensuite, furnished with curtains in Lewis & Wood's Chinese Toile. The study, a cosy masculine space, has a well-used fireplace and a collection of quirky objects.

Above: The exterior of the Victorian terrace. *Opposite*: In the sitting room there are echoes of the owners' travels in Asia. Dae silk by Manuel Canovas covers the chairs and the curtains are Montrose silk by Colefax and Fowler.

Above: A pair of black and gold silk prints is framed in mahogany above a polished wood table. *Opposite:* The kitchen-dining room opens to a neat courtyard garden.

Above: On the spacious landing a traditional elephant chair, upholstered in a stripe silk by Ralph Lauren, makes the perfect daybed. *Opposite:* The study has a decidedly masculine air with sturdy polished wood furniture, strong contemporary paintings and a well-used fireplace.

Above and opposite: The bedrooms are intimate spaces, the beds dressed in luxurious silks and cashmere. The furniture is antique and the walls are covered in paintings.

DOUBLE TAKE

A TUDOR-STYLE HOUSE WITH A CONTEMPORARY ADDITION
SEEMS LIKE THE BEST OF BOTH WORLDS

The owners of this Tudor-style period house in south county Dublin used to live in a redbrick terrace close to the city centre, a location they loved but, when they heard this unique property was up for sale, they realised they could be persuaded to move for more privacy and a bigger garden. Hidden behind high walls and mature trees, its private nature appealed. As well as secluded grounds that could accommodate a tennis court and lawn, a studio for the owner to paint in and a treehouse, the house itself was pretty and full of character. A protected structure, the owners recognised it required extending and modifying to make it work as a family home in which five children could be accommodated. Keen that the revisions would not detract from the building's fabric, setting or historical significance, they engaged a conservation architect to extend the house to provide two additional bedrooms and a modern kitchen and dining area at ground level that would open to the garden. Reached by a flight of granite steps, the door opens to a pretty tiled porch leading to an elegant hall flanked on either side by drawing room and dining room, the former with windows on three sides, flooding the room with light. A wide staircase leads to the bedroom floor. Downstairs, the original warren of small rooms has become two family rooms and a large kitchen and dining area, the contemporary design successfully blending with the period character of the house, and looking honestly of its time.

Above: The house in its verdant setting. *Opposite:* An elegant antique sofa in the bay window in the drawing room allows the detail in the room to be admired. The Great Mr Punch artwork is by Graham Knuttel.

Right: Blonde maple parquet floors throughout the formal rooms and pale walls and wallpaper allow specific pieces stand out, including the owners' collection of Irish art with works by Richard Kingston and Tony O'Malley. The wool and silk border rug from The Dixon Carpet Company in Oughterard was commissioned specially for the space. The coffee table was made from a gilt picture frame with legs turned to match. The furniture comes from various sources including auctions and vintage sales.

Above: A view from the all-white kitchen through to the dining area with cream leather chaise longue and the tennis court beyond. *Opposite:* One of the family rooms with the entire wall painted red and lined with red curtains, giving a cinema feel to the space.

Above: Elegant fitted wardrobes line one wall of the master bedroom, the lilac sofa and cream rug anchoring the restful space. *Opposite:* The cabinet in the bathroom matches the wardrobes; small bedside tables were painted in silver leaf to match the headboard surround.

PERIOD PEACE

HOME AFTER YEARS ABROAD, A YOUNG DUBLIN COUPLE COAXED A NEGLECTED PERIOD HOUSE BACK TO ITS ORIGINAL GRANDEUR

This detached Monkstown house is part of a terrace whose construction began in 1840 and spanned five years, imbuing it with details from both Georgian and Victorian eras as well as quirkier elements like Egyptian-style motifs which were becoming popular at the time. Uninhabited for years before interior designer Corinna Knaggs and her husband Trevor Dolan took possession of it in the early noughties, it lacked heating, plumbing and electrics and so the initial phase of work meant a complete overhaul of the basic fabric of the structure. While facing the reality of a derelict house, truly beautiful decorative details, almost 650 square metres of living space and a basement that could be converted to a self-contained apartment for rent, were of significant comfort. Having combated dry rot, damp and a roof in need of repair, a decision was taken to add a three-storey atrium at the rear to bring light in to slightly too-dark rooms. This addition has since been replaced by a stunning contemporary extension which also accommodates two huge bathrooms – a feature that has greatly enhanced the top two floors where the bedrooms are situated. A very cool glass bridge links this extension with the back garden to complete the spacious layout on the ground floor. Generously scaled rooms here and on the first floor face a park while further up the house the bedrooms benefit from views of the sea. With a perfectionist's eye for detail, Knaggs has spared no effort in achieving a very skilled makeover of what is now a wonderful family home (the couple has two children). With a keen sense of keeping the architectural details to the fore, there's a subtlety to the furnishing and decoration throughout although strong contemporary elements, as well as antiques, salvaged furniture, vintage finds and designer pieces have been collected over the years. Some came from Dolan's family, others from Knaggs' time spent as a designer in Chicago, as well as art from contemporary Irish artists.

Above: Corinna Knaggs at home. *Opposite:* Light pours into the hall highlighting superb plasterwork and the stunning interior fanlight. Many pieces of furniture were bought at auction and restored.

Previous pages: The inner hall with its spectacular staircase leading to the drawing room upstairs. The antique Murano glass chandelier was sourced in Italy and shipped back in pieces for the owner to assemble. The first floor drawing room has a mix of English and French furniture, its elegant windows providing a view of the sea. *Above:* The juxtaposition of old and new: a Philippe Starck Ghost chair and a pretty antique table with Bakelite telephone. *Opposite:* The kitchen on the ground floor with stainless steel island, designed by the owner and factory-made to specification.

Above: The master ensuite bathroom, with matching sinks and contemporary slipper bath, also houses a sauna. *Opposite:* A guest bedroom decorated in elegant shades of grey and white.

CONTEMPORARY ELEGANCE

SIMPLE HORIZONTAL LINES AND AN OPEN FLOOR PLAN
MAKE A HARMONIOUS FAMILY HOME

When the owners of this contemporary detached house in south county Dublin went house hunting in the late 1990s, it was the private sylvan setting within a small and exclusive group of properties that clinched the deal. They lived in the house for four years, then engaged Sheehan and Barry Architects to draw up plans for a complete remodelling. This involved the family moving out for a year while the builders gutted it, changing the layout and removing the internal walls to open up spaces and build an extension to the rear. The latter was a two-storey double-height glazed box, its cement and glass façade overlooking the garden. The extension, which accommodated an enlarged living space and a new master suite, and enabled the owners to extend the children's bedrooms to become more functional spaces with desks and seating areas appropriate for teenagers, expanded the living space by a third. Having fallen in love with the mature trees on the site, the aim was to make more of them, ensuring that the view to the garden could be accessed from all of the rooms in the house. Achieving this meant installing sliding panels between living spaces, allowing the living, dining, sitting and kitchen areas to be linked, or not, depending on the season and the mood. Very simple materials – oak boards, plain walls, natural stone – are used throughout the house, complemented by the owners' fine collection of Christian Liaigre furniture, chosen for its elegance and restraint and interspersed with pieces from B&B Italia and Poliform from Minima. Space, trees, light – the owners achieved all they wanted.

Above: The private rear garden with mature trees was the inspiration for the owners to open up the back of the house, flooding the space with light.
Opposite: An artful edit by the owners of their contemporary furniture collection has resulted in a chic interior; the sofa is by Cassina, the lamp by Flos, both from Minima. The Barcelona chair is by Knoll.

Above: When the interior was stripped out and reconstructed, an enfilade was created with the sitting, dining and drawing room spaces interlinked, yet capable of being compartmentalised with sliding partitions. *Opposite:* The open plan kitchen is a mix of concealed storage and open shelves. The sofa and pouffe are by B&B Italia, as are the dining chairs.

Previous pages: The contemporary Bulthaup kitchen from McNally Living is a mix of materials including oak, stone and stainless steel. From the mezzanine levels, a view to the dining space below. The dining table, chairs and bench are by Christian Liaigre. *Left:* Furniture by Christian Liaigre anchors the living spaces, along with some special pieces commissioned by the owners. *Below:* The master bedroom with dressing area cleverly concealed behind a floating wall which is also designed as a bedhead with two nightstands. A balcony overlooks the garden.

4

IRISH HOMES RESTORED

Aware of its architectural heritage, Ireland is keen to maintain its priceless old buildings but those houses not destined for state upkeep must rely on architects and owners to restore them to their former state, gently amending them so they can be lived in. Many beautiful houses, having lost their original lustre, have been reconstituted thanks to the loving care of a new generation of owners. Some have enjoyed meticulous restoration, others are enjoying a new lease of life where careful refurbishment has saved valuable period details and sensitive remodelling has resulted in properties that work as family homes in a modern context. Others have required dismantling of previous so-called improvements. For rescuers and restorers alike, preserving the past is a long process, requiring patience and passion. A successful result is always characterised by careful consideration of the original state of the building and a respect for the fabric of the interior.

REGENCY RESTORED

A MAGNIFICENT STUCCO HOUSE IN THE INNER DUBLIN SUBURBS
IS FULL OF PERIOD ELEMENTS FROM THE 19TH CENTURY

Dublin's Harcourt Terrace was built in the 1840s by Jasper Joly, the only example of a Regency terrace in the city. Having evaded decades of potentially disastrous planning decisions, Harcourt Terrace is now a quiet residential area with no through traffic, just a stone's throw from St Stephen's Green. The terrace of white stucco houses faces a 20th-century row of Edwardian redbricks whose aspect must be enhanced by the unique view. The Regency houses have beautifully ornamented façades and Georgian sash windows, the front doors with their teardrop-style fanlights overlooking railinged front gardens. Once upon a time, a row of lime trees was planted in the centre of the street and, although this is long gone, the owners of these fine Palladian-style houses have ensured that trees play their part in making this unique part of the city so attractive. For Pat Whyte, resident of 16 years, it was the beautifully proportioned rooms and not the prospect of a lengthy restoration process that made her decide she had to live here. As minimal structural modifications were permitted, and with the decorative stucco detailing remaining in mostly good condition, she set about repairing and restoring the damage to floors and ceilings and planning the remodelling of the basement which was to become the kitchen and living space and the main bathroom which is situated on the first floor return. The original doors were in good nick, requiring only new doormongery, and the original brass stair rail was uncovered during a process to restore the wood panelling on the stairs. Grand fireplaces needed cleaning and polishing back to their original splendour and Whyte and her husband Niall could then indulge their shared interest in architectural salvage and antiques, sourcing both here and abroad and finding furniture and fabrics that would work within the style and context of the house. Over the years, the interior has been fine-tuned with some revisions made, but the dining room and drawing rooms still come into their own when friends gather.

Previous page: The dining room with walls with antique paint effect in claret and gold. *Above:* The exterior of the Regency terrace house. *Opposite:* The elegant mahogany dining table and chairs are family heirlooms; the curtains made from an 18th-century French fabric sourced by the owner.

Above: The vestibule is painted in Regency-style eau-de-nil stripes by Michael Daly, London. The Regency gilt-framed mirror and table were found in Dublin. *Opposite:* A view to the spacious bathroom on the return.

Above: Much attention was paid to sourcing furniture and fabrics that were in keeping with the style of the period of the house. The early 19th-century French sleigh bed came with matching oval bedside tables. *Opposite:* In the master bedroom, gold raw silk, a 19th-century taffeta pelmet, dyed bullion fringing and antique tassels create a rich mix of gold and eau-de-nil. The antique trunk is by Goyard.

Above and opposite: The early 20th-century shower, originally installed in The Dorchester, London was sourced at auction for the large family bathroom which has a panelled mahogany surround for the 1830s bath. Salvaged floorboards and a deep cobalt blue on the walls add to the feel of a gentlemen's club.

GEORGIAN LUXE

A TERRACED PERIOD HOUSE IN DUBLIN GETS ITS GROOVE BACK

In Helen Kilmartin's sleekly luxurious home and former workspace in one of Dublin's picturesque canalside terraces, the seemingly impossible was achieved: the restoration of a magnificent 19th-century house, designed and decorated in comfortable contemporary mode. Kilmartin has crafted elegant modern interiors for many years, importing Italian furniture brands like Prememoria, B&B Italia, Flexform, Minotti, MDF Italia and Casamilano and showing them in a domestic setting. It was a clever approach where visitors absorbed not just the pieces they saw but gleaned hints of a very attractive way of life. Throughout Dublin's history, the banks of the canals have come in and out of fashion as places to live. Now that the capital has become so densely populated, the Georgian terraces, once the domain of offices, have a newly domestic air as families have moved in and refurbished. It can be assumed that most have been refurbished in one of two styles, either the traditional period transformation or the newly minimal stripped back space. Kilmartin avoided both, bringing to this space the kind of contemporary comfort that is very inviting. As a metropolitan space, it was intended for entertaining, studded with modern furniture and art, and planned with an urban edge. Using the hall as a smart starting point with its glossy floor, mirrored wall and crystal chandelier, the sequence of rooms unfolds. Whilst the interior was unconventional for a house of this period, the original interior divisions were maintained so no radical open plan solution was imposed. Instead, in the darkly glamorous ground floor rooms, furnished with a roll-call of smart designer pieces – Saarinen, Minotti, Castiglione and others – the mood was richly sober, the textures masculine, in contrast with the upper level where light diffused through the long Georgian windows and the palette was all creams and pale grey. At both levels, the main rooms had fine 18th-century marble functioning fireplaces, around which were grouped various pieces of modern furniture, a natural juxtaposition of old and new. What makes this house ideal for a busy life in the city? It is logically laid out, the rooms arranged to be adaptable to work and domestic life and the contents an ever-changing mix of exciting modern pieces. Although Kilmartin has moved her showroom to Hanover Quay, her home remains a great reflection of her style.

Above: Helen Kilmartin. *Opposite*: In the drawing room, curtains in a voile by Baumann filter the light through the Georgian windows. The sofas and side table are by Casamilano; the lights by Santa & Cole.

Above: In the dining area, a black lacquer table by Eero Saarinen and classic upholstered dining chairs. The cabinet and lamp are by Minotti. The paintings throughout the house are by contemporary Irish artists. *Opposite:* An antique silver gilt mirror hangs over the marble fireplace. The chair is by Paolo Navone, the lacquer table by Minotti and the bar cabinet by B&B Italia.

Above: In the hall, a chandelier by Louise Kennedy, panelled mirrors and a black stair carpet make a dramatic entrance. *Opposite:* The dark oak cabinet to the right of the fireplace is by Casamilano; the desk in the window is dark-stained sycamore with a leather inset by Hugues Chevalier.

HISTORIC ACHIEVEMENT

THE RESTORATION OF A PERFECT PALLADIAN VILLA

Set amid 1,000 acres of wood, parkland and lakeshore in Cootehill, Co Cavan is one of Ireland's finest Palladian villas, Bellamont Forest. Built in 1728 by Edward Lovett Pearce, the famous architect who also designed the former Houses of Parliament in College Green, now Bank of Ireland, the commission was bestowed by Lord Justice Thomas Coote, his uncle by marriage to Ann Lovett. Still in his twenties, Lovett Pearce seemed young to be granted such a responsibility but, by the time he completed his Grand Tour of France and Italy, his detailed knowledge of the villas of the great Renaissance architect Andrea Palladio was unsurpassed and thus Ireland reaped the benefit of his genius with two fine examples in the neo-Palladian style. The house is redbrick with ashlar facings, four bays square, built over two storeys with a basement and a Doric limestone portico. The entrance hall and saloon or ballroom have superb coffered ceilings and the central upper hall on the first floor is lit by a beautiful oval cupola, the first known example of a feature that was to become typical of Irish country houses, such as at Russborough, designed by Pearce's assistant, Richard Castle. Bellamont Forest passed out of Coote ownership in the 1870s until 1987 when the late John Coote, an Australian descendant of the Coote family, purchased the estate. An interior designer by profession, with a thriving business in Melbourne and a number of projects around the world, Coote embarked on the restoration of Bellamont Forest. He brought the perfectly proportioned rooms back to life in the decorative style of the 18th century, and imbued them with all the comforts of modern living. As well as being a home for Coote and his children when they gathered in Ireland from all parts of the world, it became the headquarters of Coote's design business. The house was furnished with brilliant replicas of 18th-century Irish furniture to Coote's specifications, from peat buckets, lanterns and fire grates to side tables and chairs. The most perfect party house, according to the late Coote, its situation in the landcape is also perfection.

Above: Bellamont Forest. *Opposite:* The dining room with elaborate coved ceiling and richly ornamented plasterwork. The furniture was created by John Coote and is based on original Irish Georgian designs.

Above: Pedimented doors lead into the formal ground floor saloon and dining rooms from the impressive entrance hall with Portland stone tiles and coffered ceiling. *Opposite:* The elegant saloon with splendid coffered ceiling, one of many rooms in the house with perfect proportions. The rug was made to a 19th-century design and all the furniture is by John Coote.

Left: The lower ground floor was renovated but the original stone-flag flooring and vaulted ceiling were restored and new cupboards and shelving added in the kitchen. The original servants' tunnel links this floor with the walled rear garden.

Top and above: Pearce's first floor toplit bedroom hall. A stone staircase leads to the central upper hall on the first floor which is lit by an exquisite oval cupola. *Right:* A comfortable guest bedroom: the painting above the bed is by Irish artist Robert Healy.

5

THE IRISH ABROAD

The range of interiors created and lived in by Irish people living abroad reveals a multiplicity of styles. Whether a restored English family home, a cool contemporary London pad or a bijou flat in the heart of Paris, a recognisable sense of culture and identity is always present, together with the influences of the adoptive cities. Although the residences are as varied as the inhabitants, all are inviting and stamped with personal style, arranged for cocooning, relaxing and entertaining guests. Some are dense with references and personal touches, others just pique curiosity with hints and subtle touches of a lifestyle. Some of the Irish abroad have a highly developed gift for composing interiors and are serial movers and doer-uppers, creating spaces that combine attention to architectural detail, decorating style and essential modern comforts, while others are simply focused on creating a place in which to live and unwind in peace. Either way, they reflect a passion for cultivating a comfortable home away from home.

TWO BECOMES ONE

LINKED BY A FLOATING STAIRCASE, TWO APARTMENTS
BECOME ONE HOME

David Collins, architect and designer, was brought up in a house by the sea in Dublin and dates his love of blue back to his pale blue bedroom in Glenageary. It's a palette that appears often in his impressive portfolio of commercial work for which he is justifiably famed: the high-profile Blue Bar at the Berkeley Hotel being just one example: Nobu, Locanda Locatelli, the Wolseley in London; L'Acajou in Sandy Lane, Barbados; the Bassoon bar and Massimo restaurants in London are others and he has many private projects worldwide. The Marble City Bar and the Set theatre in Kilkenny are two Irish projects that have attracted attention. He first had the opportunity to design a space for himself when, having lived in a conventional two-bedroom apartment in London, he managed to acquire the one upstairs, linking the two with a floating staircase and completely remodelling to create a one-bedroom, three-reception room space. Not perhaps the wisest investment but a reflection of how he wanted to live. Completed in the 1990s, its transformation has stood the test of time. According to Collins, residential projects are like haute couture, allowing him to experiment with fabrics and finishes that might be too complex or expensive to achieve in restaurants or hotels. It also allows the working of ideas on a manageable platform before he releases them to be used on a grander scale. The sophisticated blue walls in the drawing room made of canvas panels with cracked gesso on a copper leaf base are reminiscent of the Blue Bar; the convex mirror on the stairs was used at Locanda Locatelli. Shades of blue and lavender work beautifully with the tobacco brown leather sofas he designed. But the living space is not a showcase: with acoustics in mind, the walls of the music room are upholstered in silk and, intimate and luxurious, the dining room's oval ebony table and Missoni-upholstered chairs are often deployed for card games. His bedroom is, of course, blue with a pale blue leather screen, lacquer table, light and bedspread all designed by David Collins.

Previous page: The view from the music room to the bronze and perspex staircase. *Above*: David Collins at home. *Opposite*: The drawing room with white lacquer and pale blue silk lounge chairs and a travertine-topped desk in lacquer and bronze, all designed by David Collins. The 1920s ceramics on the wall, bought because they reminded Collins of Celtic swirls he saw at the National Museum, are by Primavera.

Above: The music room with Irish-made wool carpet by Vsoske. Mirrors hung on the blue silk upholstered walls are by David Collins and the photograph over the Turkish marble fireplace is by Didier Massard. A glass and bronze 1960s bar trolley is used as a coffee table. *Opposite*: The Venetian travertine fireplace was designed by David Collins. The nickel and mirror 1930s tables are by Jacques Adnet. The painting is by Christian Bérard.

Above: The Italian marble bathroom with triptych mirror hanging over the basin, is hung with photographs – changed often – from Collins' collection.
Opposite: The oval ebony table with Collins-designed dining chairs upholstered in blue and silver silk by Missoni. The 1950s lights are by Jean Royère.

Above: The master bedroom with pale blue leather screen, lacquer table, leather and silver disc light and silk appliqué bedspread, all by David Collins. The 1940s chair is by Marc du Plantier. *Opposite*: A Fornasetti cabinet with a painting of the Infant of Prague by Grillo.

CURATOR AT HOME

A RAMBLING QUEEN ANNE-STYLE LONDON HOUSE IS HOME TO A VERY PERSONAL COLLECTION

The house Polly Devlin and her husband Andy Garnett live in, in Bedford Park in Chiswick, was designed by Norman Shaw in the 1880s in the Queen Anne style. This estate, described by Sir John Betjeman as the most significant suburb built in the 19th century, was an idealistic venture with a church, parish hall, club, stores, pub and school of art. WB Yeats and Camille Pissarro lived here amongst many other artists, actors and writers. The house is large and rambling, idiosyncratic and full of light, with things one doesn't expect in a London house, like washrooms and sculleries, a drying room and cellars and a huge studio and a lodge in the garden. It was a hotel and then an oligarch's residence, at which time all the original features were removed including floorboards, fireplaces and plasterwork. When Devlin acquired it a number of years ago, she found when she walked into some rooms, lights switched on unexpectedly and music blared out alarmingly. She spent a year and a half restoring the house, including removing embedded Swarovski crystals from the walls and hidden speakers in the ceilings. She grows vegetables all year round in the kitchen garden and there is a plant house for orchids and her favourite geraniums. The house is filled with paintings and objects but it is not cluttered. As Devlin says: "Cluttered is not mindful of the space around objects. There isn't an object in my house that I don't love and treasure, and I know the background of every one." Whether it's from 17th-century France or 21st-century Massachusetts or from the smallest village in Ireland, everything has its memories and history and that is its attraction for her rather than any intrinsic value. "There's not a thing in my house that hasn't its story attached. Each thing encapsulates a time in my life – the happy place where I bought it or found it – so there is nostalgia and memory in there too." Handling each object, she says, is holding her history in her hand.

Above: Polly Devlin at home. *Opposite:* The 1950s Danish sofa is by Hans Wegner. Devlin commissioned the two stools after a pair she saw in Ham House. The large ceramic lights are by John Stefanides. Devlin has collected blue and white china over many years: the big tulip holders and obelisks are by artist Simon Pettet. She mixes the blue and white china with Staffordshire dogs so the effect is not too serious.

Above: The 1850s papier-mâché chairs are by Jennens and Bettridge; their covers are suzanis from Uzbekistan. The 1930s shell bureau is from Cap Ferrat. The marble bust of Clytie on a barley sugar column was bought at a house sale in Co Wicklow and the mysterious painting is one of a pair found rolled up in a house in northern France and painted in the 1920s. Devlin made the ceramic model of an Elizabethan house she lived in for many years. *Left:* The needlepoint ottoman was made by Garnett's grandmother over a period of 20 years – she started when she was 73. The big sofa is by John Stefanides. The glass objects on the chimney shelf were made by Serge Roche in the 1930s. The flower painting is by Vanessa Bell. The grandfather clock is from Normandy, from about 1890. Some of the cushions were embroidered by Devlin and the sculpture on the bookshelf is by Eilis O'Connell.

Above: On the desk, there is a painting by Martin Mooney and an inkwell given to Devlin by Diana Vreeland. The big painting is by Terence Flanagan, the one below it by Melita Denaro. The chair is Danish, from the 1950s. *Left*: Devlin copied the kitchen table from one in Monet's kitchen at Giverny. The tole chandelier is Irish and the ceramic figure is by Cleo Mussie.

Above: In a guest room, an English four-poster in maple, watercolours by E Wharton and Sine Mac Kinnon, a 19th-century rag rug and a Persian rug. The wooden rabbit is from Vietnam. *Right:* Beside Devlin's very high bed there is an Indian stool. The wooden Gustavian bench at the end of the bed is by Colefax and Fowler. The large painting of an angel visiting three girls by Anthea Craigmyle is flanked by paintings by Tessa Newcomb and Irish artist Una Watters. The needlepoint bedhead depicts Devlin's former home in Sussex. Above it hangs an 18th-century Chinese watercolour. The nursery rugs are from Garnett's childhood home.

STAR QUALITY

HOTEL-STYLE APARTMENT LIVING IS DESIGNED FOR A FRENETIC LONDON SCHEDULE

There's a type of living space that seems to personify every city and, for Louis Walsh, that's the one to embrace. In Dublin he lives in a period house in a leafy suburb; in Miami where Walsh has spent part of every year for the last decade, it's a space in one of the most exclusive – and the tallest – buildings on South Beach; and in London where his schedule is most demanding, it has to be the closest to hotel-style living he can get. Having been a fan of French designer Philippe Starck since he designed an apartment in the Élysée palace for François Mitterand and then partnered with Ian Schrager to completely revolutionise hotel design, Walsh loves the all-mod-cons approach to luxury inherent in hotels like the Sanderson and the St Martin's Lane, places he liked when staying in London. When a 1937 telephone exchange building in St John's Wood – named the Yoo Building after the design group who developed it – was converted to a concept created by Philippe Starck in the early noughties, Walsh was first to acquire a duplex penthouse. Like most Starck projects, it drew celebrities – pop stars, movie actors and showbiz people, all accustomed to 24-hour concierge facilities, vertical carousel parking, underfloor heating, state of the art kitchens and bathrooms and ultra high-tech audio visual systems. A decade ago, this contemporary luxe approach was completely new, now it still seems fresh: the open plan living space with daylight streaming in through floor-to-ceiling windows opens to a decked balcony and the marble and stainless steel kitchen – hardly ever used, according to Walsh, who prefers room service – makes the perfect bar for parties.

Above: The terrace is a great vantage point from which to view the city. *Opposite*: The ground floor lobby with vermilion velvet drapes, curvy baroque desk, plasma television screen and Ghost stool by Philippe Starck is a dramatic introduction to the penthouse.

Above and opposite: When Louis Walsh moved in, he chose furniture by Philippe Starck for Cassina; the white Lazy Working Sofa and Lazy Working Chair, both with integrated tables and lamps. Walsh often attends auctions, buying paintings, prints and sculptures: here, his favourite Warhol screen print of Ingrid Bergman adds a splash of colour.

Above and opposite: A marble-topped island, incorporating the rarely used hob, divides the open plan Botti kitchen from the rest of the living space. The cherrywood dining table and chairs are from Driade.

Above: Downstairs, the bedrooms are simply furnished with streamlined built-in wardrobes, contemporary beds and moulded acrylic bedside tables.

Opposite: The master ensuite bathroom with Philippe Starck fittings and Venetian mirror.

GREAT PLAIN

When Limavady-born Paula Reed and her architect husband bought their London townhouse ten years ago, she found herself applying the same simple rules to its décor that she follows in her career as a style editor for a fashion magazine. The house was put together so it would last – a great, practical family space that was also sophisticated and reflected its owners' interest in design. It had to be comfortable in a no-frills way but, having three children, Reed was also determined not to surrender completely to a child-centred interior. The drawing room on the first floor is a lovely light-filled space with floor-to-ceiling windows with working shutters – as elsewhere in the house, there are no curtains, reinforcing the overall sense of a clean, uncluttered space. The furniture reflects Reed's preference for modernist classics, like the Le Corbusier cowhide chair and the Knoll-style sofa. The drawing room opens to a study, one of its walls lined with oak shelving finished with smart aluminium strips, and filled with beloved books. With a piano by the window, it is a therapeutic space as well as serving as a home office for Reed. Bedrooms are spread over the next two floors – the master bedroom, with bathroom and dressing room, on the second; the three kids' bedrooms and bathroom on the third. Downstairs, an extension was designed so the kitchen could open onto a dining space, which, in turn, leads into the garden. Again, the emphasis is on a pared-back simplicity, with an oval marble-top Saarinen table and Eames chairs taking centre stage, and the green space outside providing the backdrop. Folding doors separating the dining room from the smart stainless steel kitchen mean that mess can be hidden away during dinner parties. For the garden, Reed chose specimen trees – yew, Acers, olive – and pots of Hostas and Skimmias to create a leafy haven, while a heated plunge pool provides entertainment for the children. On the other side of the kitchen, a family sitting room is given its vibrant character with chartreuse seating by Terence Woodgate and a deep purple rug – two bold flashes of colour in an otherwise white space. It's this balance of colour and light, design and comfort that Reed has mastered throughout the house, proving that the demands of a modern family home need not mean compromising on style.

Above: Paula Reed at home. *Opposite*: In the first floor dining room, as in the rest of the house, the oak plank floor with bevelled edge is tricky to keep but worth it for the definition it gives the simply decorated rooms.

Above: In the sitting room, the chartreuse felted wool modular sofa is by Terence Woodgate. *Opposite:* In the study is Reed's piano. The parchment star light was made by designer Tom Dixon. The shelving is oak with an aluminium strip concealing lighting.

Above: The extended dining area, with Eero Saarinen table and chairs by Charles and Ray Eames, overlooks the pretty garden with specimen trees including olive, yew, and Acer. The path leads to a heated plunge pool which, when not in use, is covered in decking. *Opposite*: The stainless steel kitchen has folding doors which open to the dining area.

BIJOU LIVING

Architect Clodagh Nolan fell in love with this dilapidated one-bedroom apartment on the prettily named rue des Rosiers in the Marais as soon as she saw it. However, the reality of buying – and restoring – a pied-à-terre in Paris is rather less romantic than the dream: as well as the practicalities of overhauling decades-old plumbing and wiring systems, Nolan had to contend with the restrictions of rebuilding within a listed 19th-century building, as well as altering the whole layout to allow space for a small second bedroom. It was a labour of love. Comprising a living room, master bedroom, guest bedroom, small kitchen and shower room, the third-floor apartment had many of its original features intact – oak parquet flooring, mouldings and plasterwork – making it a perfect candidate for a sensitive remodelling. The master bedroom is separated from the main living area by folding doors that can be left open when it is not in use, thereby creating extra room and making the most of the glorious light that floods the space. Meanwhile, the small second bedroom, originally an alcove, overlooks the quiet courtyard. While Nolan remained faithful to the classic Parisian aesthetic of the apartment, an Irish influence is evident in some of the furniture – the traditional cast-iron and brass bed in the guest bedroom and the curtains made of Moygashel linen – which she has mixed with local finds, like the carved master bed from Blanc d'Ivoire. The sleek oak and stainless steel kitchen, too, came from Ireland, built in Thomastown, Co Kilkenny. The scale of the four-month renovation meant that she could come up with an overall design scheme for the apartment, uniting all the rooms in neutral shades – mainly soft grey and off-white, enlivened by occasional touches of lavender and aubergine. Together with the carefully chosen furniture, the palette creates a restful mood of pared-back sophistication, a reflection of the city itself.

Above: With space at a premium in central Paris, thoughtful planning has created additional accommodation for guests; in the sitting room a bed-in-a-box doubles as an ottoman. *Opposite*: Paul Berg was commissioned to make the stainless steel and oak kitchen in Ireland; he then travelled to Paris to install it.

Above: Original parquet floors throughout the apartment were sanded and polished. *Right*: The French folding screen was sourced in Ireland and repatriated.

Above and opposite: Looking out over the cobbled street, the master bedroom, with its muted palette, benefits from lovely light; the baroque-style bed is from Blanc d'Ivoire, the decorative detailing on the bed repeated in the chandelier and screen.

Above: In the pretty guest bedroom, a lavender and mauve colour scheme prevails. The brass and cast-iron bed was found at auction in Ireland. *Opposite*: The 19th-century glass-fronted cabinet is used to store linen.

6

IRISH COUNTRY LIVING

The Irish country house embodies a casual, family-based way of life that has endured through generations. From the modest to the very grand, these houses display the patina of age and embody the history and character of the families who own them and often the community which surrounds them. Scuffed floorboards, battle-scarred antiques and collections of objects and equipment, from Wellington boots to fishing rods to boogie boards, eloquently express the interests of the inhabitants. The pursuits of the residents may change, but the atmosphere, of morning light coming through the windows and rainy afternoons in front of turf fires, remains the same. The Irish country house, a stalwart of Irish literature of the 19th and 20th centuries, retains its romanticism and timelessness, no matter how life around it may change. Modern houses in country settings seem at first to take a vastly different approach but, in fact, the end result is the same. Irish country living, whether in a grand house, a farmhouse, or a contemporary house nestled into the landscape, focuses on a casual and comfortable way of life where simplicity and practicality are key.

SET IN STONE

A SEASIDE FARMHOUSE IS A WELCOMING RETREAT

This handsome house on Ballyshane Strand in East Cork had been deserted for over half a century when the current owner bought it as a weekend retreat a number of years ago. The stunning location, close to the water's edge, was the deciding factor in taking on such a big project – there was only half a roof at the time of purchase – and dictated the neutral, understated style in which it was decorated, so that the beauty of the views could take centre stage. The building work took a year to complete and involved the total gutting and rebuilding of the house, which now comprises two reception rooms, a scullery kitchen and dining room, with three bedrooms and two bathrooms upstairs. Facing due south, the two identical rooms on either side of the entrance hall receive light all day long. Like the rest of the house, they are painted in Farrow & Ball shades of putty and chocolate, the room on the left functioning as a relaxed living room with large sofas and bookcases, and that on the right a slightly more formal drawing room. In the scullery, natural clay plaster walls give an authentically rustic feel, while at the back, an informal dining space, complete with Aga, opens on to the garden. Throughout, there is an emphasis on vernacular furniture, such as an old Irish bookcase and the large dresser in the dining room. Upstairs the four original bedrooms became three: the first of these, off the return landing, contains two sets of bunk beds, providing ample accommodation for weekend visitors. Up again, a guest bedroom and ensuite master bedroom at the front of the house mirror the two rooms below, with wonderful views over the sea and surrounding countryside.

Previous page: In this country house in Co Cork, a plain limestone fireplace and natural floor covering provide a simple backdrop for an antique portrait. *Above*: The period house is perched on the coastline. *Opposite*: The sitting room with the owner's collection of furniture acquired at auction. The coffee table is roughly covered in Donegal tweed.

Above: Simple objects, beautifully arranged, give the interior an eclectic feel. *Opposite*: Polished wood, natural floor coverings like sisal and seagrass and loose covers in muted shades add to the sense of relaxed comfort.

Above: A view from the sitting room to the living room; the dark painted doors add definition and drama. *Opposite*: The kitchen with its original fireplace opening and new French doors to the garden. The traditional-style old pine trestle table and chairs look perfectly at home.

Above: Throughout the house, simple tongue and groove wood panelling is used effectively. *Opposite*: The owner keeps things simple in the bedroom with an old painted bench and an Irish wool blanket on the bed.

Above: Poultry have the run of the gravelled courtyard where house guests gather for lunch on sunny days. *Opposite*: A traditional scullery is practical and reminiscent of the days when mod cons were unheard of and every dish was washed by hand.

KEEPING THE FAITH

A FORMER BISHOPS' RESIDENCE, ARDBRACCAN WAS
LOVINGLY RESTORED TO ITS FORMER GLORY

The grandeur of Ardbraccan, a Palladian-style mansion in Co Meath, is testimony to its one-time status as the residence of the Bishops of Meath. The imposing limestone structure that stands today was commissioned in 1734 from Richard Castle, the architect behind Russborough and Leinster House, and completed over 30 years later with contributions from other architects. But when the current owners came into possession of it in 1998, Ardbraccan was in great need of restoration, having lain empty for a time. The painstaking work took over four years – the plasterwork alone requiring 18 months to strip and clean. The results are stunning: on the ground floor, a vaulted entrance hall leads to an enormous central saloon at the rear of the house. Opening off this are the main reception rooms, including a library, resplendent with deep red wallpaper, a drawing room and dining room. Upstairs, on the first floor, the main bedrooms are occupied by the family, while the original servants' quarters on the top floor have been transformed into a series of elegant guest suites. The complete overhaul extended to the basement level, where a flagstone floor was laid, and a large, warm kitchen created. Also off the long vaulted corridor is a bright, airy laundry room. The decoration throughout was the work of the interior designer Serena Williams-Ellis, an expert in historic houses, together with the owner of the house. The furniture is a mix of auction finds and inherited pieces. While remaining faithful to its heritage, there is a relaxed informality to the new Ardbraccan, in keeping with its main purpose – that of a welcoming family home.

Above: The unadorned garden façade dates from the 1770s, the grey of the limestone heightening its austere impression. *Opposite*: The ground-floor library, with its deep red walls and Kilkenny marble fireplace. The recessed glazed mahogany bookcases are from the 18th century.

Above: The central saloon has the proportions of a ballroom. The round mahogany table at its centre was inherited from the owner's grandmother. Above the fireplace hangs an 18th-century landscape. The ornate plasterwork in this room was painstakingly restored over 18 months. *Opposite:* The light colour scheme of the drawing room, with its hand-printed wallpaper, enhances the natural daylight that pours in through the large windows.

Above: In a guest room, an antique painted chest stands at the end of the brass bed. *Right:* At the foot of the bed in the master bedroom on the first floor is an 18th-century sofa, while above it, an antique textile wall-hanging from Central Asia adds a touch of colourful exoticism.

Above: In the basement, a large, airy laundry room that runs the length of the vaulted corridor. The flagstones on the floor were found in Belfast. *Opposite*: The wonderful original stable buildings have also been restored, with the old tack room serving as a home for the children's bicycles and other odds and ends; along the walls are the original fittings.

NATURAL SELECTION

IN SYMPATHY WITH THE SURROUNDINGS, NATURAL MATERIALS
AND OPEN SPACE ARE USED TO GREAT EFFECT

When architect Kim Dreyer and his wife Susan were hunting for a site on which to build a new house, they came upon this peaceful space in the gentle Co Wicklow countryside, surrounded by mature trees with glimpses of hills beyond, and knew their search was over. The cedar-fronted two-storey house is approached via a gravel drive fringed by mature trees. The bedroom "wing" is housed to the front and an intimate hallway opens to a light-filled glazed link connecting to the rear of the structure, a sequence of smaller spaces culminating in a grandly-proportioned open plan living space that leads – through a series of timber French doors – to a sunny paved courtyard. This rear part of the building is also clad in cedar, this time painted soft white, with a reclaimed slate roof. Kim Dreyer, who studied architecture in Copenhagen, the US and India, was determined to put an eco-friendly stamp on the plans and made a conscious decision to use materials that become more beautiful with age – oak and limestone, sculptural concrete, green oak trusses from local wind-felled trees. Heated geo-thermally, the house is effortlessly low-energy with heat drawn from the ground on which it sits, while eco-paint and sheep wool insulation help create a healthy indoor climate. This is a graceful house, a combination of both grand six metre-high ceilings and intimate spaces, closely connected to its surroundings. It accommodates hectic family life and lots of entertaining, and affords opportunities for quiet contemplation.

Above: Susan and Kim Dreyer at home. *Opposite:* The kitchen-dining area, overlooked by the mezzanine, with chairs by Charles and Ray Eames surrounding a beech and steel dining table, designed by Kim Dreyer and built by a local cabinet-maker.

Above: The living area, viewed from the mezzanine, with leather Balzac sofa by Matthew Hilton, and modernist-style sofas designed by Kim Dreyer. In the corner is an antique Vietnamese food chest. The green oak coffee table, designed by Kim Dreyer, was made from wind-felled timber from the area.

Above: The mezzanine, an informal space from which to enjoy views of the Co Wicklow countryside, has lots of built-in storage space and seating.

Above: Stone steps lead from the entrance hall to the living area and a view of the limed oak staircase which leads to the mezzanine and bedroom levels.

Opposite: The west-facing sun room with deep built-in lounging area and sandstone floor has a Mediterranean feel, the glass pivoting doors opening to a sandstone courtyard, making one seamless sun-filled space.

MODERN EXPRESSION

A TRUE MODERN CLASSIC, THIS COUNTRY HOUSE COMBINES
18TH-CENTURY STYLE ELEGANCE WITH THE COMFORT OF A CONTEMPORARY HOME

The grand scale of this spectacular house in the South East might lead one to make assumptions about what lies behind its imposing façade. However, the owners, who have farmed the surrounding land for generations, were determined to make it a comfortable family home rather than a look-but-don't-touch museum piece. Although hard to believe, the house is a new build, completed on the site of an older structure that burned down in the 1920s. Its site and aspect were determined by the 18th-century landscaping, including the avenue of mature lime trees by which the house is approached. Creating an abundance of light was a priority for the owners, and full-length windows along the front of the building allow it to pour in, also providing wonderful views of the avenue and lush countryside beyond. The house, designed by the late John Coote, is divided into two wings, with a staircase at the centre, rising from the airy entrance hall to the bedrooms on the first floor. On the ground floor, an enfilade of rooms reflects the progression from private quarters to entertaining spaces, with relaxed family rooms situated at one end and more formal dining and drawing rooms at the other. Much of the furniture was custom-made, so that it would be in keeping with the grand scale of the high-ceilinged rooms. Again the emphasis is on comfort and function rather than a rigid formality, and although there is a distinctly period feel to the interiors, paintings and rugs and occasional modernist pieces add a dash of contemporary style. The most dramatic room in the house is also, paradoxically, one of the most intimate – a double-height library with mezzanine – and a glass-roofed conservatory is another wonderfully inviting space. Beyond this are two guest suites, while the corresponding wing on the other side houses a large kitchen and utility rooms – all working together to create an elegant, welcoming family home.

Above: Designed to fit in the footprint of an earlier building, the new house looks as though it has always belonged at the end of the avenue of lime trees.
Opposite: The galleried entrance hall, with its polished limestone floor, features a brass lantern and mahogany circular table, both custom-made for the space by Coote and Co. Many new pieces recall the past, like the peat buckets made to an 18th-century design.

Above: Generously proportioned sofas and chairs, an open fireplace and a leather ottoman make the family room an inviting space. *Opposite*: The double-height library is one of the most impressive spaces in the house, with a book-filled mezzanine accessed from the first floor. The bespoke light fittings were designed by John Coote and, while the mood is relaxed and traditional, an Eileen Gray glass and chrome side table adds a touch of modernity.

Previous pages: While elsewhere in the house, a laid-back mood prevails, the dining room is slightly more formal, and the picture of restrained elegance. Pale gingham chair covers and a cool palette serve as a counterpoint to the dark mahogany of the table and sideboard. The bespoke porcelain dining service was also designed specifically for the owners by Coote & Co. *Above:* Inside the stables – creating a home for the many family pets was another priority for the owners. *Opposite:* It was easy to create an open plan space for the kitchen, given the generous proportions of the ground floor.

A NEW COUNTRY

OVERLOOKING THE MULLINGAR COUNTRYSIDE, THIS HOUSE COMBINES AN
AMBITIOUS MINIMALIST AESTHETIC WITH THE DEMANDS OF RURAL FAMILY LIFE

On a hill overlooking Lake Derravaragh in Co Westmeath, encircled by an ancient oak forest, is a stark and dramatic modern house, its scale and daring becoming apparent only as the long drive nears its end. It was thoughtfully designed for owners Deryn Mackay and Mark Fagan by architect Neil Burke-Kennedy around their differing lifestyles – she in the fashion world, he an equine vet and horse trainer. While the structure seems at first to be uncompromisingly contemporary, Burke-Kennedy's firsthand experience of the couple's lifestyle translated into the adoption of many typically rural features, including the accessible boot and coat room, the two-storey structure and the drive-in yard. As in all classic country houses, the countryside comes right up to the house – no suburban-style landscaping was permitted. The house is built on a northeast-southwest axis, the front overlooking the six-furlong all-weather hill gallop where Fagan's horses train, the back with wonderful views of the lake. The structure is essentially a rectangular box, with robust painted plaster walls and two rectangular apertures, one framing the entrance, the other balancing it. The interior of the ground floor is open plan with kitchen, dining and living spaces flowing into each other. There is an abundance of glass and the house is full of light at all times of the day, in every season. Mackay's love for minimal decoration and a neutral palette is evident in the design scheme, which was devised with the help of interior designer Bill Simpson. It proved a highly effective partnership: Simpson introduced elements of black and helped sub-divide the large ground floor space to make it easier to live in. The traditional and modern are juxtaposed. Although an Aga has been installed, the windows remain curtainless, in keeping with the minimalist façade.

Above: The contemporary country house. *Opposite*: The entrance with ha-ha in front to prevent animals straying into the house, a traditional alternative to a wall or electric fence in keeping with the minimalist architecture.

Above: Lots of glass allows for great light and wonderful views of all aspects of the site. The sculpture separating the dining and living area is by Patrick O'Reilly. The painting on the right is one of several in the house by Guggi. *Opposite*: In the family living room, complete with open fireplace, the wenge coffee table introduces an accent of black, Mackay's favourite colour.

Above: Given Mackay's fashion background, colour and texture play a large part in the decorating scheme as evidenced in this relaxed seating area, with its sophisticated palette of gold and black. *Opposite:* The kitchen in walnut and black granite. The Aga is the only typically traditional feature in an otherwise contemporary room – but, according to the owners, it's a necessity.

Left and opposite: Bedrooms are dressed simply, in restful tones. *Below:* There is a spectacular view from the main bathroom.

FAMILY SEAT

The Clandeboye estate, presided over by Lindy, the Marchioness of Dufferin and Ava, a member of the Guinness family by both birth and marriage, is one of Ireland's oldest and covers over 2,000 acres in northern Ireland. Known locally as Ballyleidy, the house, an early Georgian mansion, dates from 1801 and was built by Robert Woodgate, an apprentice of Sir John Soane, who was commissioned by Sir James Blackwood, 2nd Baron of Dufferin and Ava. The two-storey mansion with two wings built at right angles with a single-storey four-columned Doric portico is surrounded by intimate walled gardens, pasture for the estate's award-winning Holstein and Jersey cattle, and extensive woodland gardens. When the Marchioness, daughter of Loel Guinness, married a distant cousin from the brewing side of the family, Sheridan Hamilton-Temple-Blackwood, 5th Marquess of Dufferin and Ava, she was to move into a house that was already stamped with the character of Frederick, the 1st Marquess, over 80 years before. He inherited at the tender age of 15 and with a lifelong fascination for architecture, continued to adapt, alter, embellish and add to Clandeboye during his lifetime. The 1st Marquess was a favourite of Queen Victoria and a trusted diplomat whose career meant that ongoing projects in relation to Clandeboye – including the construction of an indoor tennis court and bowling alley and the addition of a banqueting hall and museum room – were interspersed with his requirement to travel. Stints as Governor General of Canada and then as Viceroy of India allowed his passion for collecting to flourish. Clandeboye is home to the extraordinary gifts presented to him on his travels and there are reminders everywhere of his influence. Bedrooms are named after places the first Marquess was sent "en poste", the rooms are full of treasures brought back from east Asia, and collections of weaponry, heraldry and hunting prizes line the walls. The Marchioness and her late husband's determination to preserve the unique character of the house and ensure its ongoing self-sufficiency has been achieved, magnificently.

Above: Lady Dufferin at home at Clandeboye. *Opposite:* The wonderful library with bookcases inscribed in gilt with the names of the Greek gods. Sir Harold Nicolson, nephew of the 1st Marquess, described the library as "one of the pleasantest rooms on earth".

Previous pages: In the inner hall, weaponry, heraldry and hunting prizes line the walls. Egyptian sculptures, Burmese wood carvings, stuffed grizzly bears and rhinoceros heads as well as many other remarkable treasures and curiosities were brought back to Clandeboye by the 1st Marquess of Dufferin and Ava, one of the Victorian era's most brilliant ambassadors. As newlyweds, Lady Dufferin and her late husband Sheridan began to catalogue the 1st Marquess's vast collections and continued to restore and improve the house, buying fine furniture and paintings to replace pieces that had been damaged over the years or were sold off during two world wars. *Right:* The large billiards room is lined with bookshelves.

Above: The staircase, flanked by a pair of Icelandic narwhal tusks and decorated with artefacts collected in east Asia, all souvenirs from travels by the 1st Marquess, during his time as diplomat and ambassador. *Opposite*: The dining room with sideboard laden with candelabra.

Previous pages: The dramatic entrance to the inner hall with deep red drapes and a pair of stuffed bears (acquired by the 1st Marquess while Governor General of Canada) guarding the way to the baronial-proportioned space, the stained glass window representing the arms of the families linked with Clandeboye. Over the fireplace hangs the portrait of the 1st Marquess of Dufferin and Ava. The Chapel of Clandeboye was the private chapel of the Blackwood family. *Above:* The drawing room overlooks the park. *Opposite:* Lady Dufferin, a successful artist who uses her maiden name, Lindy Guinness, works in a light-filled studio at Clandeboye, formerly the drawing room.

Above and right: The names of the bedrooms at Clandeboye reference the many places where Frederick Hamilton-Temple-Blackwood, the 1st Marquess of Dufferin and Ava, served in his ambassadorial role, among them France, Russia, Canada, India and Italy. This guest bedroom, named "Paris", is richly decorated with pattern, colour and gilded furniture.

7

REMOTELY IRISH

It is only when the mist descends and soft rain falls or the landscape is windswept and battered by the elements, that a cosy, warm and interesting interior comes into its own. The traditional home in the Irish countryside tended to turn its back on the environment, its orientation conservative, its windows small and its priority shelter. With the focus on conserving heat and staying warm, kitchens and sitting rooms were functional cosy spaces. For those who chose to restore and refurbish these properties, it was often necessary to open them up, to bring in light and to create family spaces more conducive to modern living. But for newly designed rural homes the point became about panorama, making the most of the view, whatever the season. Sensitively sited and conceived, the modern rural house is a pleasure to live in and to look at, but so often the impact on the landscape has not been benign. Bold contemporary approaches to design were more successful than pastiche but there are many abominations of both genre. In the following pages, positive aspects of both old and new are celebrated, the shared characteristic being an interior that communicates well with the exterior and the surrounding landscape.

A NEW NOBILITY

BUILDINGS OLD AND NEW INFLUENCED THE DESIGN FOR THIS COUNTRY HOUSE

Ballyedmund House was designed in the 1980s by architect Professor Cathal O'Neill for one of his children. Located on a sloping site at the southern end of a long 50-acre densely wooded property, it has extensive views south, east and west over east Co Cork. The house was designed to reflect the siting of a typical early Irish house, reminiscent of the formal placement of 18th-century dwellings – a plain and simple form standing proudly in the landscape. On a platform of in-situ concrete, a steel frame with a large expanse of glass on the southern side is combined with zinc panelling and concrete walls extended to the other side. The accommodation is stacked on three levels with a central entrance hall two storeys high, and a gallery at the upper level. The main living space with entrance hall, kitchen, dining and drawing rooms is on the middle level. The children's and guest bedrooms are at ground floor level with the main bedroom, dressing room and bathroom and a guest room and opera hall on the top floor. Every room has windows to the south, with the hall and top floor rooms also having windows to the east or west. Terraces surround both upper floors. The deep overhanging roof, supported by freestanding steel columns within and outside the structure, restricts the sun's penetration in the summer months when the light might be glaring, yet in winter it facilitates the low sunlight. Internally, the rooms are arranged symmetrically around the double-height hall and, with the exception of a door leading into the kitchen, the space is completely open plan.

Previous pages: This light-filled modern family home takes its place in the landscape. *Above*: Professor Cathal O'Neill with family on one of the large terraces that surround both floors of the house. *Opposite*: The French limestone which covers the entire floor at entry level is a seamless reflection of the terrace outside.

Left: An early evening view of the house showing the children's and guest bedrooms and the solid base at ground floor level with the main living space – entrance hall, kitchen, drawing and dining rooms – on the middle level. The top floor contains the master bedroom, bathroom and dressing room, a guest room and opera hall.

253

Above and opposite: The master bedroom, looking south from the west terrace, has a stunning view over east county Cork, providing an almost gallery-like space which, being at the top of the house, is not overlooked.

CLEAN SLATE

A TRADITIONAL FARMHOUSE IS GIVEN A NEW LEASE OF LIFE
THROUGH A THOUGHTFUL RENOVATION

Nestled into a hillside in Co Kilkenny, with the Blackstairs Mountains visible in the distance, this 19th-century farmhouse and its cluster of outbuildings have been been brought back to life through a sensitive conversion by the architect owner, who has transformed them into a restful family getaway. Having lain derelict for over ten years, the house was in need of a complete renovation, and while the resulting building has a contemporary feel, it remains faithful to the original structure both in layout (the adjoining outbuildings remain in their original positions, as do the windows) and in the spare, unfussy interiors. The main house is entered by a traditional half-door, the narrow entrance hall leading to a guest bedroom on the left, and a bright kitchen on the right. Blue limestone floors and pale walls maximise an abundance of light in the kitchen, which is the hub of life within the house, and the uncluttered mood is enhanced by a few thoughtfully chosen pieces of furniture – a vintage Danish bread cupboard and a salvaged pine table. Beyond the kitchen, a small gallery leads to a wonderful double-height living area – originally a barn – with a mezzanine loft, accessed by a ladder, that is pressed into service when extra guests come to stay. Bathed in light, this space is also home to some wonderful pieces of Irish art. Upstairs in the main house, the understated mood is carried through the two generous bedrooms and large bathroom in a palette of pale blues and off-whites. Off to the other side of the house, accessed via the exterior deck, a studio provides another relaxed seating area, the rough-hewn stone walls and sloping ceiling a reminder of the original outbuilding, and of the harmony the owner has managed to create between the old and the new.

Above: The exterior of this converted farmhouse in the heart of the Kilkenny countryside is largely unchanged from its original incarnation but inside, the architect owner has created a modern, contemporary holiday home. *Opposite*: The original barn was turned into a double-height living area, with a central stove, and an old-fashioned orchard ladder leading to the mezzanine.

Left: The pine kitchen table is flanked by simple director's chairs. *Right*: A green painted zinc-topped vintage French cabinet provides a quirky touch. *Below*: The studio, separate from the main house, echoes the original building, with its exposed masonry walls and reclaimed radiators. As elsewhere, a cool palette of blues and neutrals creates a calm mood, while light pours in through the skylights overhead.

Above: The master bedroom – like the rest of the house – is furnished simply but tastefully, with a French painted cupboard and a rosewood sleigh bed.
Opposite: The bathroom, upstairs in the main house, with its painted wood-panelled walls. The windows on this level are low, almost at floor-level, due to the higher level of the new floor.

COLLECTOR'S RETREAT

A BEAUTIFULLY SITUATED HOUSE IN THE WEST HAS A UNIQUE CONTEMPORARY CHARACTER

For many years, the owners of this Connemara house were guests of designer Ros Walshe and her husband, artist Patrick Walshe in their rented holiday home in Claddaghduff. Following one particularly lovely summer there, Jim and Jan Shore began the search for their own property, a place where they could come every year from their base in South Carolina. It had to be big enough to have friends to stay and sufficiently versatile to be cosy and comfortable at Christmas and New Year, yet light and bright enough to bring the outdoors in in summer. Ros Walshe was tasked with the research, eventually finding Stream End, a beautifully situated one-storey modern house not far from Clifden. The unique setting, combined with the fact that no structural work was needed, clinched the deal, and Shore and Walshe, with their shared lifelong love of collecting objects and antiques, immediately set about planning the look for the interior. While beautifully designed to take advantage of the ever-changing landscape, the interior was just too minimal and streamlined for Shore's taste. The first decision was to begin work at the heart of the house, redecorating the dual-aspect kitchen to give it a country, yet contemporary, air. Walshe arranged to have the work surfaces sanded back and the walls repainted in White Tie by Farrow & Ball. This alone was enough to remove the modern edge and, when the collections of objects were added, the French chandelier hanging over the vintage farmhouse table, and the cupboard handles replaced, the transformation was almost complete. All that remained was for Walshe to plunder her collection of antique numbers to number each and every cupboard, a brilliant and practical idea she borrowed from her mother, Mary Mason-Jones. The games and music room, completely sound-proofed thanks to the previous owner, a sound engineer, is where the kids hang out, playing music and watching movies and where Shore's collection of antique toys is hung on the walls. Above it is the loft, where the children sleep and into which no adult ventures until it is time to clean up and depart. In the sitting room, a narrow modern fireplace surround has been replaced with an old stone window sill and sofas are covered in a faded floral chintz and Shore's collection of antique patchwork fabrics mixed with tweeds. In the study, salvaged school honours boards and in the hall, an old industrial tool bench add character and interest. For the bedrooms, Walshe and Shore continued their search for interesting pieces in antique markets in France, finding wall lights and battered leather chairs as well as old mirrors and pretty antique knobs for doors and drawers. In winter, velvet curtains from Ikea create a cosy interior but it is in summer when this house comes into its own and the stunning views of the mountains and the sea can be appreciated to the full.

Above: The house in the ever-changing Connemara landscape. *Opposite*: In the living room a pair of 1930s French office lights and a collection of trophies from antique fairs hang over the faded floral sofa with cushions covered in tweeds and vintage linen.

Above: In the hall, a zinc-topped timber chest was found at a market in France as was the pair of table chandeliers. *Opposite*: A collection of needlepoint tapestries was framed and hung in the hallway; the oil painting is by Patrick Walshe.

Above and opposite: One of the previous owners, a keen chef, planned the spacious kitchen; the new owners took the edge off its modern look by sanding the wooden countertops, replacing the cupboard door handles and repainting with a softer paint palette from Farrow & Ball. A grouping of restaurant cloches is another attractive use for one of the owners' many collections of objects. The weathered kitchen table and chairs are 18th-century Scandinavian.

Left: Amongst the many collections gathered by the owners is one of traditional toys, chosen for their craftsmanship; the collection of push-along dogs became so extensive the owner had to hang some on the wall.

SPORTS
CHAMPIONSHIP CUPS.
BOYS.

	Senior	Junior
1922	HOWARD, R.V.	SMITH, A.T.
1923	{HEMMING, D.E.E.	BEATT, H.A.
	{WHEELER, M.	
1924	MOASE, G.	DOUGLAS, A.J.
1925	HARVEY, E.W.	BROAD, C.
1926	HARVEY, J.P.	HALL, J.B.
1927	CLARK, R.H.	McLEOD, J.
1928	BROAD, C.L.	COUSINS, J.
1929	BROAD, C.L.	WRIGHT, K.T.
1930	BROAD, C.L.	WRIGHT, K.T.
1931	COUSINS, J.	BROWN, S.C.E.}
		MILES, M.K.}
1932	WRIGHT, K.T.	MILES, P.J.
1933	EBERT, F.A.	INGHAM, R.G.
1934	GAGE, R.W.	LIPSON, G.E.
1935	MILES, M.K.J.	LIPSON, G.E.
1936	MILES, M.K.J.	LAILY, C.G.B.
1937	PERKIN, R.H.	CHAPLIN, D.
1938	CROSBY, B.C.	CAMPBELL, J.A.

Left: The open plan study – with salvaged school honours boards on the wall – links the kitchen with the hall. A pair of Lloyd Loom chairs dates from 1939.

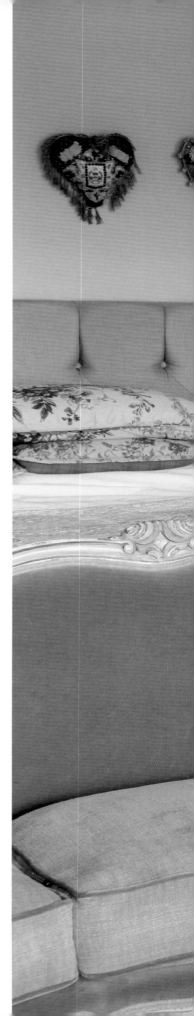

Above: Blue and white is a favourite combination: in the guest room, floral and stripe linens are combined to great effect. *Right*: The master bedroom with French marble-topped walnut chest, sofa in blue-grey trimmed with taupe velvet and French wall lights. The oils of flowers were collected in junk shops all over the world.

ROCK STEADY

THIS CONTEMPORARY HOME IS PERFECTLY IN TUNE WITH THE LANDSCAPE

Derrynane, on the western edge of the Ring of Kerry, is an area of such astounding natural beauty that any development must abide by strict rules on everything from building materials to style and a "traditional" aesthetic is preferred by the powers that be. But architect Donogh O'Riordan, of Cork-based O'Riordan Staehli Architects, found a way to create an utterly modern building without breaking the rules and disturbing the natural landscape. When O'Riordan first encountered the site, he was determined to incorporate the small quarry that had been excavated in the creation of a local access road. The result is a house built from slate and local stone that seems to nestle between two mounds that veil it from the outside world. The house itself is built into the quarry, so that although it might look, from one angle, like a single-storey house, below the original ground level is another floor, including three bedrooms. The upper floor is largely open plan, an airy space with white walls accentuated by splashes of vivid colour in the internal porch that separates living and dining areas as well as the recesses that contain the staircase and a small library. The effect is more like that of a modern city apartment than a rural retreat. It's the perfect setting to hang exciting art, and a piece by Gwen O'Dowd from her An Uimbh series competes for a visitor's attention with the truly astonishing view of the majestic Skellig Rocks. The upper floor also includes the master bedroom, which shares the spectacular views, and the study, a soothing space with circular window looking into the living area that provides a tantalising glimpse of the sea beyond. Downstairs, the three bedrooms (one of which has an ensuite bathroom) share the beautiful views, framed to perfection by the natural mound on the east and the artificial one to the west. All these rooms face south (the more utilitarian rooms, such as the bathrooms, all face north), allowing not only the sea view but the advantage of constant sunlight (or as constant as Irish sunlight can be) during daylight hours. Outside on the eastern side, a spacious deck, accessible from the upper floor, extends over solid rock, sheltered from the wind by the mound that rises above. Like the rest of this beautiful house, it all seems to blend effortlessly into the wild and beautiful Atlantic coastline.

Above: The two-storey house nestles into the landscape, the lower half set in the quarry, with mounds of earth built up on either side of the entrance, concealing the full extent of the house. *Opposite:* The tranquil sitting room, with painting by Gwen O'Dowd.

Above: The interior, although thoroughly crisp and contemporary, is made very inviting with the use of striking red in the dining area. *Right:* A warm yellow on the stairwell wall is balanced with tones of green and blue chosen for furniture.

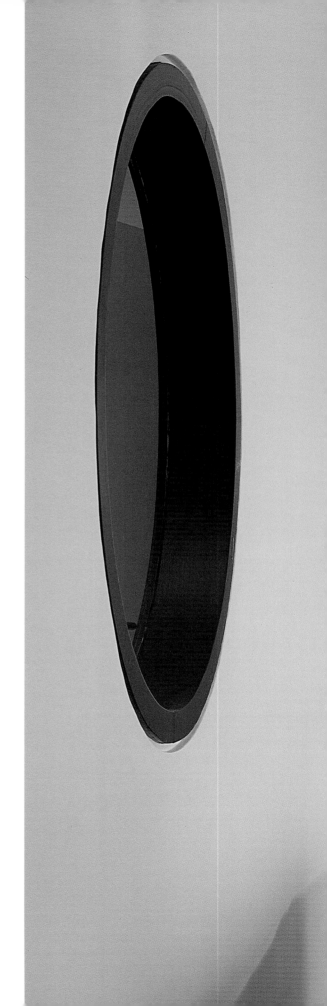

Above: Taking full advantage of the views, the entrance and main living areas, as well as the master suite, are on the first floor with additional bedrooms and bathrooms at ground level. The wood-burning stove is positioned so that the views can be enjoyed even on chilly days. *Opposite*: The view framed with wooden blinds.

ACKNOWLEDGMENTS

THIS BOOK IS DEDICATED TO RANDAL AND BETTY McDONNELL
FOR THEIR LOVE AND INSPIRATION.

We would like to express our thanks to all those who helped with the creation of this book, especially the owners and interior designers and architects of the houses that are featured and to one special owner, Polly Devlin, who accepted our invitation to write the foreword. Our thanks to Catherine Heaney for her invaluable help in the early stages and to Siobhán Kennan who assisted with copy editing and Karen Howes whose familiarity with the photography archive meant that thousands of images could be retrieved and sorted easily. Our gratitude also to Sinéad Leahy who first worked with us on the design of the book and to Jane Matthews who shaped it into what is is today. Our sincere thanks to our colleagues at Gloss Publications, to art director Laura Merrigan, and Aislinn Coffey, Tracy Ormiston, Lynn Enright and Sarah Halliwell.

Originally published in 2012 by Gloss Publications Ltd,
The Courtyard, 40 Main Street, Blackrock, Co Dublin, Ireland.
www.thegloss.ie

ISBN 978-0-9567005-1-3

GLOSS PUBLICATIONS